FOREWORD

Making distilled spirits at home is as satisfying and rewarding as any hobby for those who live in countries where it is legal to do so. Homebrewers and winemakers would find it particularly interesting because it is a logical extension to their present hobbies. There are the same mashing and fermentation stages as in brewing, but instead of drinking the brew, it is subjected to a purification process. The process is distillation, a process as fascinating as mashing and fermentation are.

This is not a hobby for everyone, but no hobby is. In the first place you would only wish to become involved if you particularly liked the beverages it produces. Secondly, you should enjoy the challenge of constructing a scientific apparatus that involves a little plumbing and a little electrical work.

The satisfactions you receive will include the knowledge that you are restoring an art that was such a pervasive part of early Americana, and yet is all but completely lost on modern society. And finally, there will be the pleasure derived from making a beverage, pure corn whiskey, which is in every way as excellent and respectable a spirit as the finest whiskies and brandies well known to the connoisseurs of today.

American Distilling Institute

White Mule Press, a division of
American Distilling Institute
PO Box 577
Hayward, CA 94541
distilling.com/publications/books

Copyright 2023 © Ian Smiley BSc
All rights reserved.
978-1-7369802-7-9

DEDICATION

> **I dedicate this book to my wife
> Eleanor
> whose help and support were
> invaluable to its completion**

CONTENTS

CHAPTER 1	INTRODUCTION	1
CHAPTER 2	**PURE CORN WHISKEY**	3
	Beer and Wine	3
	Distillation – what is it?	4
	Simple Distillation	5
	Fractional Distillation	5
	Whiskey, Brandy, Rum, etc	6
	Pure Corn Whiskey	7
CHAPTER 3	**THE HISTORY OF CORN WHISKEY**	9
CHAPTER 4	**EQUIPMENT**	23
	The Mashing Vessel	24
	The Fermenters	24
	Ancillary Equipment	25
	Refractometer	25
	Hydrometer	25
	Proof Hydrometer	25
	Hydrometer Cylinder	26
	Proof Hydrometer Cylinder	26
	pH Meter	26
	pH Papers	27
	Transfer Hoses	27
	Immersion Chiller	28
	Spirit Still	31
	Material of Construction	32
	Construction	33
	The Boiler	34
	Thermostat	35
	The Heating Element	36
	Electrical Timer	37
	Potentiometer	38
	Attaching The Reflux Column	39
	The Reflux Column	40
	Stillhead	41
	Liebig Condenser	42
	Heat Exchanger	43

	Packing	47
	Filling and Draining the Spirit Still	48
	Other Considerations	49
	Beer Stripper (Optional)	50
CHAPTER 5	**INGREDIENTS**	**55**
	Corn	55
	Malt	56
	Water	58
	Yeast	60
	Glucoamylase	62
	Calcium sulphate ($CaSO_4$)	64
	95% Sulphuric Acid (H_2SO_4)	64
	Calcium Carbonate ($CaCO_3$)	65
CHAPTER 6	**MASHING**	**67**
	Principles	67
	Mash Water	68
	pH	68
	Measuring pH	69
	Adjusting pH	69
	Temperature	70
	Iodine Starch Test	70
	Procedure	71
	Equipment	72
	Ingredients	72
	Method	72
CHAPTER 7	**FERMENTATION**	**75**
	Principles	75
	Grain Mash Fermentation	76
	Fermentation Times	76
	Specific Gravity (SG)	77
	Measuring SG	78
	Calculating Alcohol Content	80
	Straining the Mash	80
	Procedure	82
	Ingredients	82
	Equipment	82
	Method	82

CHAPTER 8	DISTILLATION PRINCIPLES AND PRACTICES	87
	Principles	87
	Whiskey Distillation	91
	Foreshots	92
	Heads	92
	Middle-run	92
	Tails	92
	Feints	93
	Operating Procedures For Distillation	96
	Transferring the Mash to the Still	96
	Transferring the Low-wines to the Still	97
	Measuring Alcohol Content	97
	Beer Stripping	98
CHAPTER 9	DISTILLATION METHODS	101
	Fractional-Distillation Method	104
	Flow Rate	109
	Diluting	110
	Blending	110
	Storage	111
	Pot-Still Method	112
CHAPTER 10	SUMARRY OF PROCEDURES	115
	Mashing	115
	Fermentation	115
	Beer-Stripping Distillation	116
	Spirit-Run	116
CHAPTER 11	PURE-ETHANOL DISTILLATION	119
	Procedure	120
	Diluting	126
	Storage	127
CHAPTER 12	OTHER WHISKEY-MASH RECIPES	129
	Thin-Mash Recipe	129
	Mashing With Backset	131
	All-Grain Malt Whiskey Recipe	132
	Equipment	134
	Ingredients	134
	Method	134

Malt-Extract Recipes 136
Thin Malt-Extract Recipes 137
Wheat Malt-Extract Recipes 138
Peat-Smoked Malt Recipes 138
Bourbon-Mash Recipes 140
Rye-Mash Recipes 140
Corn-Squeezins' Whiskey 142

CHAPTER 13 **TRADITIONAL SOUR-MASH WHISKEY** 145
Principles 145
Procedure 148
    Equipment 149
    Ingredients 149
    Method 1 –
        Intermittent Sour-Mash Cycle 149
    Method 2 –
        Continuous Sour-Mash Cycle 153
Other Considerations 154
    Rhizozyme (Koji) 154
    Bacterial Contamination 155
    Yeast Mutation 156

CHAPTER 14 **MAKING YOUR OWN MALT** 157
Making Barley Malt 158
    The Grain 158
    Steeping the Grain 159
    Germinating the Grain 159
    Drying the Malt 160
Making a Wooden Kiln 162
Making Corn Malt 164
    The Corn 165
    Steeping the Corn 165
    Germinating the Corn 165
    Drying the Malt 166

CHAPTER 15 **OTHER MASHING METHODS** 169
Flaked Grains 169
Cereal Grains 169
Method 170

	Equipment	170
	Ingredients	170
	Millet	171

APPENDIX A	**TEMPERATURE CORRECTIONS FOR HYDROMETERS**	173
APPENDIX B	**PROOF-HYDROMETER TEMPERATURE CORRECTION TABLE**	175
APPENDIX C	**SPIRIT-RUN RECORD**	179
BIBLIOGRAPHY		181
INDEX		183

x *Making Pure Corn Whiskey*

CHAPTER 1

INTRODUCTION

Numerous books have been written on homebrewing and home winemaking, and some have even been written on home distillation to produce pure ethanol for making: gin; vodka; and essence-based spirits, but very few have been written on distillation for making whiskey and other flavour-positive spirits on the small scale required by hobbyists. This book has been written in an attempt to rectify this situation, and to accommodate the recent advent of micro-distilleries and distillery pubs that are reintroducing the art of making corn whiskey and other grain whiskies made famous by the early frontier folk.

This book should appeal to readers who have no experience with brewing or fermentation, as well as readers who do. A basic knowledge of the simplest forms of all-grain brewing is definitely an asset, but not a necessity. All the mashing, fermentation, and distillation principles are explained in sufficient detail for the novice to learn everything they need to know to produce the finest pure corn whiskey.

Also, this book gives a brief history of corn whiskey and how it was the pivotal industry that sustained the early settlers who opened up the American frontier. The history not only serves to remind the reader of corn whiskey, but of the rich culture, strong principles, and self reliance that are at the foundation of American society, of which corn whiskey was such an important part.

The temperatures in this text are quoted in °C followed by °F in brackets (eg. 65.5°C (150°F)). Often the °C temperature will be expressed to one place of decimal. This is not done as a matter of precision but because most of the °C temperatures quoted are translated from °F, so in order to remain equivalent to the °F temperatures some will need to be expressed to one place of decimal.

Also, the temperatures quoted in the procedures are the optimum temperatures and every effort should be made to adhere to them. However, variations of a degree or two either way would not result in failure of a process, but rather a slower reaction, or the production of more non-fermentable sugars and less fermentable ones, etc. In other words, a slightly less than optimum result, but otherwise perfectly workable.

Before getting down to the details of mashing, fermentation, and distillation a few general observations will be made in the next chapter on the subject of what pure corn whiskey is and of alcoholic beverages in general.

PURE CORN WHISKEY

All alcoholic beverages are made by fermenting a sugar solution (a.k.a. a fermentable substrate) with yeast, a process that converts the sugar ($C_6H_{12}O_6$) to ethanol (C_2H_5OH) and carbon dioxide (CO_2). Usually, one does not start with a pure sugar-and-water substrate, but with fruit juices for wine, mashed grains for whiskey, molasses for rum, and many others. Regardless of the sugar source the alcohol is the same.

In addition to the variations imposed by the source of sugar, the yeasts themselves and the conditions under which they are used also make their contribution to the character of the final product. This is because yeasts produce small quantities of other substances known as "congeners" in addition to the main product, ethanol. It is no wonder, therefore, that the flavour, colour, aroma, and general quality of fermented beverages vary so widely.

No alcoholic beverage (with the possible exception of vodka) consists simply of alcohol and water with no other constituent present. If it did, it would be colourless, odorless, and tasteless. The colour, aroma, and flavour of beers, wines, and spirits are due to the congeners present.

Beer and Wine

Alcoholic beverages can be divided into two broad categories according to whether or not there is a distillation stage following fermentation. Beer and wine fall into the non-distilled category whereas whiskey, rum, brandy, gin, etc. have all been distilled. The latter are often referred to as "spirits" or "hard liquor".

Wine and beer are produced by fermenting their respective substrates (ie. fruit juices for wine, grain mash for beer) with yeast, then clearing, aging, and packaging the fermented substrate as the finished wine or beer.

Distillation – what is it?

Distillation is simply the heating of a liquid to the boiling point followed by condensing the vapours on a cold surface back into a liquid. To remove the hardness from water it can be boiled in a kettle and the steam that is produced condensed against a cold surface to give pure water free of minerals and dissolved ions. The calcium and magnesium salts that constitute the hardness remain behind in the kettle. Nature carries out Her own distillation in the form of rain. The sun evaporates water from the surface of lakes and oceans leaving salt and impurities behind. Clouds form, condense, and a close approximation to pure water falls to Earth.

So distillation is not a mysterious subject, nor is it threatening. It is as commonplace as a rain-shower or a kettle boiling and causing condensation on a nearby window.

As you can imagine, the actual practice of distillation as a controlled procedure is a little more complicated than this and later chapters will provide an exact description of how to build the equipment required and the procedures involved in operating it.

There are actually two different types of still, the choice of which to use depending on the level of purity required in the product. Traditionally, whiskey is made in one type, a pot still. It's rather simple in design because only a moderate level of purity is required. Gin and vodka production on the other hand requires a more sophisticated type of still called a fractionating still because a very high level of purity is desired. A detailed description of the two types will be provided in *Chapter 8 Distillation Principles and Practices* because it is quite important for the reader to appreciate the differences.

However, in this text the high-separation type of still is chosen over the traditional pot still for making whiskey because of the exacting control it affords over the level of separation. High-separation stills can be operated in a manner whereby they give much less than maximum separation, which is exactly how they are very efficiently used to make whiskey. This is covered in detail in *Chapter 8 Distillation Principles and Practices*.

An advantage that falls out of this is that the high-separation still can also be used to produce pure ethanol for making gin and vodka. For a well-written text on how to do this read, Nixon and McCaw *The Compleat Distiller*, www.amphora-society.com. The high-separation still design described in this text can be used to make gin and vodka exactly as described in *The Compleat Distiller*. The distillation of pure alcohol is also discussed below in *Chapter 11 Pure-Ethanol Distillation*.

Simple Distillation

As mentioned before, the fermentation of sugars derived from grapes, barley, corn, potatoes, molasses, milk or any other source produces a wide variety of chemicals, the major one being ethyl alcohol (ethanol). Minor constituents will be propyl, butyl, and amyl alcohols. These minor constituents are collectively called "fusel alcohols" (in the past they were called "fusel oils", but they're not oils they're higher alcohols). They are responsible for the unpleasant side effects of drinking such as headaches and hangovers.

When such a mixture is distilled, the first vapours to come over will be rich in the more volatile components such as methanol and acetone. This first fraction is referred to as the "foreshots". There is no sharp separation so, long before the foreshots are completely exhausted, the ethanol begins to appear but is collected into a "heads" phase to buffer the transition between the foreshots and the beverage alcohol. Later, when the ethanol phase is tapering off, the "tails" begin to emerge. These are the least volatile components of the mixture. At first, come the less volatile esters, and then the propyl, butyl, and amyl alcohols known as fusel alcohols. Thus, in a simple distillation using a pot still there are four main fractions: the foreshots; the heads; the middle run; and, the tails. The middle run is mainly ethanol with trace amounts of heads and tails, the amount of each depending on where the cuts are made.

Fractional Distillation

As mentioned above, simple distillation of a mixture of liquids does not produce a clear-cut separation of the various components. If such a separation is required it is necessary to resort to the use of a fractionating column. The theory and practice of this will be described in detail in a later chapter but a few words will be said about it here. The procedure involves the use of a vertical column attached to the top of the boiler. The column is packed with inert particles such as short lengths of glass tubing known as Rashig rings, ceramic "saddles", wire gauze, or in fact any non-reactive material with a large surface area.

The vapours from the boiling liquid pass up the column, are condensed to a liquid at the top, and run back down through the packing in the column. This counter-current flow of vapour up and liquid down has the effect of producing a series of mini distillations at the surface of each piece of glass or metal in the column. It is equivalent to carrying out a simple distillation in a pot still and then redistilling the product over and over again. The final result is an almost perfect separation of the mixture into its various components, allowing each one to be drawn off in sequence from the top of the column in the order of its boiling point. Thus, the most highly volatile components emerge first while the least volatile components emerge last.

Whiskey, Brandy, Rum, etc.

The distillation of these products is done using a pot still or a special-purpose fractionating still, and this effects only a crude separation of the fermented substrate into foreshots, heads, middle-run, and tails. The skill in making a palatable whiskey consists of: mashing the grains into fermentable sugars; fermenting the mash under conditions that give rise to a certain mixture of chemicals; and, distilling the mixture and discarding a portion of the heads and a portion of the tails.

The middle fraction, consisting chiefly of ethanol, will also contain the retained portion of heads and tails (ie. the congeners). It is these congeners that impart the characteristic flavour and aroma. At this point there is no colour. Colour is imparted by storing the spirits in oak barrels for a number of years, a process that also modifies the chemical make-up of the whiskey to give unique characteristics of a particular distiller.

Pure Corn Whiskey

Corn whiskey is the whiskey produced by mashing corn (ie. using malt enzymes to convert its starches to sugars), fermenting the corn mash with yeast, and distilling the fermented mash. The mashed corn produces a particular profile of congeners that characterizes the flavour of corn whiskey.

Historically, the distillers of corn whiskey took pride in the tradition of producing whiskey and made their whiskey entirely from grain and malt. But, with the advent of the prohibition (U.S. 1921-1933) there was a surge of new distillers who had no particular attachment to whiskey making as an art or historical tradition. These new prohibition distillers became notorious for stretching their corn mash with sugar. Some recipes were less than 10% corn, the rest being sugar and water. While using sugar to produce a "thin mash" will produce as much alcohol and with much less effort, the flavour of the finished whiskey is different, and has less character of the grain. This prohibition type of corn-whiskey production became so prevalent that whiskey made from pure grain (ie. no sugar) became a rare delicacy, and was attributed the name "pure corn whiskey". Unfortunately, when the prohibition ended these sugar recipes persisted into the subsequent generations of corn-whiskey distilling so the traditional pure corn whiskey remained a scarce commodity.

Note: Commercial whiskey producers are bound by law to use all grain in their mashes, and no spirit made with sugar can be called "whiskey".

For a more detailed account of the history of corn whiskey during the prohibition read, Joseph E. Dabney, *Mountain Spirits*, Asheville NC, Bright Mountain Books.

CHAPTER 3

THE HISTORY OF CORN WHISKEY

This chapter, which chronicles the evolution of corn whiskey, is summarized from Joseph E. Dabney's authoritative book on the Appalachian moonshine culture, *Mountain Spirits*[†].

Mountain Spirits is highly recommended reading if you are interested in a more detailed history of corn whiskey.

To appreciate the roots of American whiskey distilling, which was born in the Appalachian frontier in the 1700s and 1800s, we must trace back to our Scottish, Irish, French, German, and English ancestors who brought the distilling art to North America over two centuries ago.

The first distillers in Western Civilization were probably the famous old Arabian and Egyptian alchemists who were trying to discover the elixir of life, which was supposed to impart long (or eternal) life, health, and youth. The first alembics (distilling pots) were built in Egypt, and the term "alcohol" is derived from the Arabian term "al-kohl", which is described as a material produced by refinement. One of the popular heroes of the subsequent distillation saga was an Arabian alchemist, Abou-Moussah-Djafar-Al-Sofi (nicknamed Geber), who lived around 700 AD and who put the distillation principles to paper. Ironically, the Arabs were prohibited by their religion from drinking alcohol.

When distillation was first discovered, it was considered by the Europeans to have been a revelation from God. Indeed, for many years after reaching Italy, Spain, and the heart of Europe, the secret of distilling was hoarded by the monks in the monasteries for those who were closest to God.

[†] *Mountain Spirits*, published originally by Scribner and now in paperback, along with its companion volume, *More Mountain Spirits*, both published by Bright Mountain Books, Asheville, NC

The result of distillation was dubbed "aqua-vitae" (water of life), and was revered as a highly prized wonder drug dispensed by the monks, alchemists, and the apothecarists. Then from aqua-vitae we go to whiskey. The popular beliefs are that the distilling secret went from the Arabians to the Spaniards (possibly by the invading Moors in the 8th century) to Ireland where whiskey was invented. Another theory is that St. Patrick brought the secret back to Ireland from Egypt around 400 AD where he learned it from the famed alchemists.

But then, St. Pat wasn't Irish. He was a Scottish Lowlander born at Dumbarton near the Firth of Clyde, where he lived until he was kidnapped by Irish Celts at age 16 and spirited away to Northern Ireland, which in a way would give the credit for whiskey to the Scots.

The question of who invented whiskey, the Scots or the Irish is disputed to this day and will probably never be settled. However, there is no doubt that Ireland and Scotland were both in the vanguard of the distilling saga and that it was in those countries that the name "whiskey" came into being. The Gaels of the old Ireland called it "usquebaugh", Gaelic for aqua-vitae. From this it became "uisge-betha", "uisge", and then simple "whiskey". The ancient Irish called their early whiskey "poteen" (pronounced put-cheen), which means, small pot.

In nearby Scotland, whiskey was highly admired and extensively manufactured as early as the late 1400s. While grain spirits were known in the Scottish Highlands and its Lowlands to the west as "usquebaugh", the early Scottish distillers, just as the Irish, had their more familiar colloquialism, "poit du", meaning black pot.

The Scots traditionally have spelled "whisky" without an "e", right to this day. So do the Canadians. The Irish and Americans spell it with an "e". Just why this is so, nobody seems to know.

This leads us into considering that hardy race of people, the "Scots-Irish" of Ulster, or "Ulster Presbyterians". The Scots-Irish brought corn whiskey making to America. More than anyone else, they popularized it, despite the mighty inroads of "rumbullion" (rum).

King James I, the first joint king of the two countries to come from Scotland, planted Scottish Protestants in the province of Ulster (the ten counties of the Catholic Northern Ireland) beginning in 1610. The intent, in part, was to make the "wild Irish" more peaceful. Just before James' predecessor, Queen Elizabeth I, had died, her British troops had finally brought the rebellious Irish in Ulster to heel after having literally burned and starved them into submission. At that point, Ulster's two clan chieftains, the Earl of Tyrone (Hugh O'Neill) and the Earl of Fyrconnel (Red Hugh O'Donnell), who had led the bloody rebellion with the backing of the Pope and with the help of troops from Spain, fled to France. With their departure, almost three million acres (1.2 million hectares) of land reverted to the British crown.

With the flight of the earls, King James gave his support to the expanded plantation idea, hoping "that the sea-coasts of Ulster might be possessed by Scots, who would be traders proper for his Majesty's future advantage." Doubtless he also envisioned the opportunity to spread the Protestant faith to Ulster. The Scottish lairds who received big land grants from James drew thousands of willing settlers from the ranks of the poor across the Lowlands, who leapt at the opportunity presented by the Ulster land. The Lowlanders could get on a 31-year "feu", virtually a lifetime lease. Under general circumstances that were far better than those available under the caste system in Scotland. Further, social order did not operate so rigidly in Ulster. Immigrants, however lowly in station, considered themselves "royal colonists". They could live where they pleased, could own a gun, could distil and drink their corn whiskey without interference (that is, before it was subjected to an excise), and perhaps most important of all, they could worship as and where they pleased, which meant, of course, in the Presbyterian "kirk".

By 1640, there were 40,000 Scots in Ulster, drawn mainly by economic opportunities. Additional thousands came in succeeding years because of religious freedom.

Now, it was during the Ulster colonization that the English Parliament adopted excise laws on spirits, mainly to raise money to finance the suppression of the Civil War which broke out in 1642. With the advent of this excise, smuggling of spirits in Britain became rampant. In addition to what they already knew, the Scots-Irish learned everything possible of the distilling art from the renowned Irish poteen makers.

During their years in Ulster, the Scots learned to drain the marshy bogs, converting former wasteland into fertile farms. The city of Belfast became a monument to Scottish enterprise. The deep-water port was literally carved out of the bog, becoming Northern Ireland's centre of export and import. The Scots introduced the potato, and, with the help of newly arrived Huguenot Protestants from France, who were great industrial technologists, they developed booming woolen and linen manufacturing industries.

But all of these industries were soon in dire straits, because the English industrial and agricultural interests could not stand the competition. Parliament was persuaded to enact laws that in effect eliminated the exporting of goods and livestock from Ulster.

Of all the harsh penalties to hit the Ulstermen, "rack-renting" was the worst. The Scottish proprietors, who had benefited from the great improvements made by their tenants, "screwed up" and "racked" the rents to double and triple their previous amounts. The Scottish-Irish farmers, feeling a sense of injury, refused to accept the outrageous rack-rent. The new leases therefore went to native Irishmen. The intransigent and dispossessed farmer had an alternative of leaving the country, to either go to Scotland, or to cross to America.

As a result, America beckoned. After only five generations in Ulster, the Scots-Irish were ready to move on. And move they did, bringing with them to this country an almost pathological thirst to own land, a strong Protestant faith, and a great tradition of whiskey making and free trading.

The first big wave of Scottish-Irish immigration began about 1717 when Lord Donegal led the way in rack-renting his Ulster tenants in County Antrim, which was followed by four other waves of immigration, and continued until 1776. It is estimated that a quarter million Scots-Irish poured into America during the five heavy waves of the great migration. While they landed at many ports from Boston to Charleston, most of them came into Philadelphia, New

Castle, and Chester, flocking into Pennsylvania and its "three lower counties" which were to become Delaware.

As pioneers, the Scots-Irish proved their mettle. They were a new kind of settler, the real pioneer, who brought strong convictions to America, including a love of whiskey and a love of liberty.

To say that the drinking and the making of liquor came naturally with the American frontier would be an understatement. To the colonist, suspicious if not deathly afraid of the "poisonous" water of the New World and faced with the reality of the rugged frontier, strong drinks were a dire necessity. From the earliest days at Jamestown, the colonists up and down the seaboard looked on alcoholic beverages as essential for survival.

It was only natural, therefore, that brewing and distilling would command an early and important role in the New World. The Virginia Assembly in 1623 called on all newcomers to bring in malt to brew liquor to tide them over until their constitutions became accustomed to Virginia Water.

By 1625 two brew houses had begun operation in Virginia. Several years earlier, an Episcopalian missionary, Captain George Thorpe, had learned how to convert Indian maize into liquor and had set up a crude distillery at Berkeley Plantation on the banks of the James River. To a friend in London he wrote that he had found a way "to make so good a drink of Indian corn as I protest I have diverse times refused to drink good strong English beer and chosen to drink that."

While Indian corn (ie. the everyday North American food-grade corn) was destined to become the base for the true blue American drink, the first spirits made and consumed in volume in America came from the fruits that grew wild and from the lush orchards that soon proliferated under the hands of the early day Johnny Appleseeds.

In the years leading up to the migration of the Scots-Irish to the American frontier in the 1700s, the early Americans began making wine from pumpkins, grapes, currants, elderberries, and parsnips. Indeed, it appeared there was no fruit or grain that was not "grist for the mill" to satisfy the colonists' desire for fermented and/or distilled spirits. They were distilling ardent spirits from blackberries, persimmons, plums, whortleberries, sassafras bark, birch barks, corn stalks, hickory nuts, pumpkins, the pawpaw, turnips, carrots, potatoes, and small grains.

Towards the late 1600s, apple cider, applejack, and apple brandy became the staple alcoholic beverages of New England and south along the eastern seaboard. In every colony, breweries and distilleries sprang up, most of them on individual farms. The stillhouse, usually a windowless log cabin, became an important appurtenance on many plantations in the South and on the farmsteads of Pennsylvania, Maryland, Delaware, New Amsterdam, and New England.

One basic role of spirits in the early days of the colonies was as medicine. Settlers drank spirits to prevent malaria and to speed the recovery of anyone taken ill. Whiskey was to the pioneer what tranquilizers, stimulants, disinfectants, vitamins, rubbing alcohol, and anesthetics are to us today.

During the years leading up to the Revolutionary War, rum became *the* distilled drink of Colonial America. Rum was consumed in many forms, from straight to mixed with cider or beer to mixes with sugar, water, and nutmeg. Some rum drinkers even plunged red-hot loggerheads into their tankards of "flip", a rum, beer, and sugar combination. By the early 1700s, the colonists were consuming twelve million gallons of rum per year.

Despite its ascendancy, rum began losing ground to the increasingly popular corn and rye whiskey coming from the American frontier. Throughout the colonies, the pioneers had been perfecting the distilling of corn.

It is about this point in time that we rejoin our friends, the Scots-Irish from Ulster.
Down the Great Valley of Pennsylvania and Virginia, through the 1730s to the 1770s, rolled one of the greatest movements of people in American history, people who were destined to change the drinking habits of the North American continent, and more important, play an important role in opening up the western frontier and waging the War of Independence.

The majority of the Scottish-Irish immigrants headed to the wide open Southwest, the great American frontier of Virginia, the Carolinas, Tennessee, and Georgia. Between 1720 and 1775, some two to three hundred thousand Ulstermen got off ships at the Delaware River ports of Chester, New Castle, and Philadelphia, and most of them swung down the verdant Great Valley of Pennsylvania, continuing into the Valley of Virginia, today's Shenandoah Valley.

By the time of the Declaration of Independence, Virginia Valley was well populated, and North Carolina's backcountry had sixty thousand settlers. Anson, Orange, and Rowan Counties, North Carolina, which in 1746 had less than a hundred fighting men, had blossomed to at least three thousand by 1750. North Carolina Governor Tyron reported that in 1765 alone, more than a thousand immigrant wagons passed through Salisbury. Neighbouring South Carolina had eighty-three thousand people on its backwaters.

Wherever the Ulsterman went, he took his whiskey. Pennsylvania's Dr. Benjamin Rush put down some disparaging descriptions of the fellow Presbyterians he had observed on a tour of the frontier. He blamed what he felt were the Ulsterman's indolent habits on the ever-present stillhouses. Rush blamed whiskey making for all of the Ulsterman's troubles, including his quarreling ways, his unkempt farms, and stump-filled fields. He reported that the Scot-Irishman loves spirituous liquors, and eats, drinks, and sleeps in dirt and rags in his little cabin.

What Rush did not acknowledge was that whiskey making had a very practical purpose for the Scots-Irish. A settler's first job on arriving in the wilderness was to clear enough land for his cabin and then get in a crop, usually corn, which was easy to produce with only a hoe. Food wasn't a problem because the forests abounded with wild game of all sorts and the rivers were full of fish. What the settler needed was a cash crop to enable him to pay his taxes and thus retain his precious property, usually a few hundred acres. This was where his whiskey-distilling became an extremely important adjunct to his farming. With their whiskey, they had "legal tender" to pay their taxes and obtain the few necessities that they could not make for themselves, such as salt, nails, and cloth. Many Scots-Irish had brought along their copper worms and small pot stills slung under their ark-like wagons, or on their packhorses. Some, however, brought only a knowledge of how to build a rig, and some, not even that. They quickly learned from one of their neighbours.

The fact that the settler was locked within the fastness of great mountain chains was another reason why it was almost inevitable that he would turn to whiskey-distilling. For although they could produce from forty to sixty bushels of corn per acre (and sometimes more on rich bottom land), it was virtually impossible for them to get ground cornmeal or flour to markets on the seaboard. They could easily and economically convert their corn or rye into spirits, however, and then with a packhorse, transport the liquid equivalent of twenty-four bushels of corn. A packhorse could carry eight bushels of grain, which would fetch about two dollars, not enough to cover the transportation cost. However, a packhorse could carry two eight-gallon kegs of whiskey, which would fetch at least 16 dollars. Practically every farmer, therefore, made whiskey.

The frontiersmen found "whiskey farming" sensible, no different from turning corn into pork, or, as in the case of his compatriots in New England, harvesting syrup from maple trees.

By the mid-1700s, columns of steel blue smoke poured from hundreds of stills over the six-hundred-mile backcountry along the Appalachian Mountain chain. "Where there's smoke, there's bound to be whiskey" was the favourite expression of the time.

Across the western frontier of Pennsylvania during the final days of the Revolutionary War, a strong full-bodied whiskey called "Monongahely rye" was becoming famous and became well known back east in Philadelphia and even down the Ohio and Mississippi Rivers. In Philadelphia, it commanded a dollar a gallon, and was recognized as hard currency much more stable than the continental dollar. Easily divisible, and constantly increasing in value as it aged in oaken kegs or sloshed around on a trip over the mountains or down the Ohio River, it was indeed the frontier farmer's greatest bank balance. They could easily barter their whiskey for the necessities of life, for salt at five dollars a bushel, or nails at fifteen cents a pound. With enough whiskey, he could buy a farm.

Every fall, the farmer-distillers of the Monongahela River County around Pittsburgh would put together mule trains and traverse the

Alleghenies via the rutted Forbes Road. Strapped across the back of each animal would be two eight-gallon kegs of whiskey, 24 bushels of grain in liquid form, 128 pounds in all (each gallon weighing eight pounds). No wonder that practically every farmer became a "whiskey grower", converting his surplus grain into spirits.

Stills made by the coppersmiths of York, Lancaster, and Philadelphia proliferated on the frontier, particularly in southwest Pennsylvania. By 1790, of the 2,500 known distilleries in operation in the 13 states, 570 were concentrated in the four counties around Pittsburgh, 272 in Washington County alone. Hugh Brackenridge, the famed Pittsburgh lawyer of the era, declared the still was "the necessary appendage of every farm, where the farmer was able to procure it". A complete copper still and worm was literally worth a 200-acre farm within ten miles of Pittsburgh. Although not every farmer could afford a still, there was at least one in every settlement, with from six to 30 families sharing its output.

Now in 1790 word got around that the Secretary of the Federal Treasury, Alexander Hamilton, had devised a new scheme to pay off the country's 21 million dollar war debt: he would tax whiskey distilleries and whiskey production! The shock waves reverberated through the backcountry, riveting the frontiersmen with rage.

Instead of receiving the appreciation due its soldiers for their heroic role in the fight against England, the West found itself confronting a discriminatory excise on its whiskey. Why didn't the federal government open up river trade with the Southwest via the Ohio and Mississippi Rivers? Why didn't it build some good roads to the eastern markets? No. What it planned to do was equivalent to a slap in the face.

Despite the West's protest and the opposition of many politicians, Congress paid no heed and on March 3, 1791, voted Hamilton's proposal into law. As amended later in an attempt to mollify the westerners, the tax was set at seven cents per gallon of liquor produced, or 54 cents per gallon capacity of each still. Adding insult to injury, the law also offered rewards to "informers" who would spy and report on unregistered stills.

This law provoked a furious reaction, and many incidents began to occur, which included gangs going around destroying the stills of the few distillers that acquiesced and paid the excise.

The most significant event revolving around the excise was the Whiskey Rebellion, which started with such a roar, and ended with a whimper. The frontiersmen formed a rebellious force of over 5,000 insurgents and descended on Pittsburgh ready to put the torch to the town, but the towns folk met the throng at the town limits, bearing whiskey and wagonloads of dried venison, bear meat, hams, and poultry, all designed to discourage a rampage through the city. The hospitality worked, and the threat of serious violence was subjugated.

Certain citizens of Philadelphia, particularly George Washington and Alexander Hamilton, were not smiling over the ominous turn of events. At Hamilton's urging, President Washington called on the governors of Maryland, Virginia, Pennsylvania, and New Jersey to draft armies for the job that lay ahead. Some 13,000 troops, including 11,000 infantrymen, were put on alert by the four governors, awaiting one last attempt to settle the issue without marching.

Washington sent commissioners to Pittsburgh, and it was agreed to hold a referendum asking the anti-excisers to submit to the new law by pledging oaths of allegiance. Those who signed would be pardoned for past offences. But the Westerners resented the oath, and the percentage of people who signed was far from overwhelming. Washington, under pressure from Hamilton, feeling no other recourse was left to him, ordered the troops to march.

Meanwhile, in Monongahela County, as the government forces swelled, the ranks of the rebels became contrastingly thin. Some 2,000 insurgents quickly disappeared from the area, among them, most of the ringleaders of the rebellion. Many fled down the Ohio River into Kentucky and beyond.

On November 13, 1794 the government troops squashed the rebellion, and numerous arrests were made. In the end, Washington pardoned all who were arrested and the rebellion was over.

The rebellion cost 1.5 million dollars to squelch, much more than the total excise collected in a year's time. But the effort apparently had the effect that Hamilton desired: it gave credibility to the power of the federal government.

But the settlers did not stop making whiskey during the excise years. Indeed, the rebellion helped set the stage for the beginning of America's widespread distilling activity, for it pushed whiskey making deeper into the West and South, into Kentucky and down the Appalachians into the Carolinas and Georgia. Many a Monongahelan lashed his still onto a pack horse and headed for the promised land, where people could carry out "stillin" to their hearts' content away from the prying eyes of the excise man.

Soon almost every farm down the Appalachians and into Kentucky and Tennessee had a still of some type. Many farmer-distillers had two copper pot stills, a large one for the first run (ie. a beer stripper), usually 150 to 200 gallons, and a smaller one (ie. a spirit still), around 50 to 80 gallons, for the second since less volume was required for the doubling run (spirit-run).

In 1794, the British gave up their northwest posts and in 1795 Spain signed Pinckney's Treaty, allowing Americans to ship their whiskey and other products down the Mississippi. These developments added considerably to the Kentucky and Tennessee boom. In just two months of 1795, upwards of 30,000 people crossed the Cumberland River into middle Tennessee. Soon, 20-ton barges were plying the Tennessee River from east Tennessee, loaded with barrels of frontier spirits, destination: New Orleans.

Meanwhile, across the "southwestern" frontier (today's southeastern U.S.) deep into Virginia, the Carolinas, Georgia, Kentucky, and Tennessee, the great common denominator was corn. It provided hoecakes and hominy for the settlers, feed for the hogs and horses and, perhaps most important, the base for the settlers' favourite drink. Moreover, corncobs could be used as fuel and shucks to fill a mattress.

Getting the corn ground presented a problem, but the frontiersmen weren't long in meeting the challenge. "Grist" mills sprung up on many a stream, alongside waterwheels. Looking back on it, it seems a miracle that the people on the frontier came up with such contraptions. But the mountain people were ingenious. They had to be. There were scarcely any roads, and they could only carry in what could be packed on a horse. The water-powered gristmills became one of the real milestones of Appalachian Americana. Like the stillhouse, the gristmill became a commodity landmark and a centre of activity.

Many historians give Reverend Elijah Craig, a Baptist preacher, the credit for discovering bourbon whiskey. In 1781, he set up a gristmill at Royal Spring in what is today Scott County, Kentucky. He employed his surplus corn and rye meal to make whiskey (bourbon, by today's Federal Government definition, is comprised of at least 51% corn and a large adjunct of rye). The story goes that he happened into storing his whiskey in charred oak barrels by using a barrel that had been accidentally burned on the inside and subsequently discovered its lubricious effects on the whiskey. Charred oak purges the clear whiskey of many of its impurities and gives it an amber colour, plus a smooth oak-flavoured bouquet and body. Today, charring the oak bourbon barrels is a federal requirement for the maturing of bourbon (minimum three years). Other accounts attribute the charred barrel to early coopers who burned straw inside new barrels to clear them of rough edges, splinters, and bacteria. Still others say that barrels were burned originally to clear out the rank odour of fish or molasses.

Regardless of how the corn-rye mix or the charred oak barrel came to be, they formed the definition of bourbon whiskey, and other styles of American straight whiskey. Today, the U.S. Federal Government regulation for Straight Bourbon Whiskey is: a whiskey made from a mash of at least 51% corn; distilled with the emerging distillate at no more than 160 proof; and aged in new charred white oak barrels for a minimum of two years.

The excise years were drawing to a close. In 1800, a significant year for whiskey distillers everywhere, but particularly for those on the southern and western frontiers, Democrat Thomas Jefferson, with the great support of the democratic peoples of the West, won an overwhelming victory over the Hamiltonian Federalists and became President. One of Jefferson's early objectives was eliminating the "infernal" whiskey excise, which he felt was hostile to the genius of a free people. Craig and his fellow whiskey distillers across the West and South celebrated the repeal, which came on June 30, 1802.

So the frontiersmen at last were free from the excise. And, except for a three-year imposition of a tax following the War of 1812, they had a relatively long era without visits from gaugers, excisemen, and collectors. This reprieve lasted until 1862. During this happy period, they refined their distilling as well as American whiskey.

CHAPTER 4

EQUIPMENT

Generally, whiskey is made in gooseneck or pot stills. Pot stills are too rudimentary in design and do not afford sufficient separation of the mash compounds to make a good quality whiskey. For this reason, they are never recommended for the production of beverage alcohol anymore.

Gooseneck or whiskey stills have been used for centuries for making whiskey and are used just as much today as they have ever been. Some of the world's finest whiskies are made in such stills, and some artisans argue that the finest whiskies can *only* be made in this design of still.

However, the operation of gooseneck and whiskey stills is very temperamental and subjective, and requires a great deal of skill to maintain a careful balance of heat and flow rate. Commercial whiskey distillery operators require years of training and experience to become accredited distillers.

A lot of whiskey nowadays is produced in special-purpose fractionating stills. These stills are high-separation stills that can separate out each compound in a mash by virtue of its boiling point. The level of separation in such stills can be very precisely controlled up or down and their operation is much more consistent and systematic than whiskey stills. And, it is because of these characteristics that the high-separation fractionating still design has been chosen for making whiskey in this text.

A secondary advantage that arises from using a fractionating still is that it can also be used to produce pure alcohol for making vodka, gin, and essence-based spirits. The method for doing this is detailed below in *Chapter 11 Pure-Ethanol Distillation*. An excellent book on this subject is: Nixon & McCaw, *The Compleat Distiller*, www.amphora-society.com.

More will be said about stills in *Chapter 8 Distillation Principles and Practices*.

The components of the distillation equipment described here can be purchased from domestic hardware stores and plumbing suppliers. They need some modification and adaptation, but the task is well within the capabilities of the average handyman.

As for scale of operation, the equipment and procedures described in this book are based on a mashing and fermentation unit of 30L (8 US gallons) of corn mash to yield about 2L (2.1 US quarts) of 40% alc/vol corn whiskey and about 700mL (¾ US quart) of 60% alc/vol feints. Feints will be explained in *Chapter 8 Distillation Principles and Practices*.

There are four major equipment items. They are: the mashing vessel; the fermenter; the beer stripper (optional); and the spirit still.

The Mashing Vessel

An excellent mashing vessel for producing 30L of corn mash is a 34-40L (9-10 US gallon) stainless steel stockpot with an aluminum plate bonded to the bottom, and a lid. This can be purchased at restaurant-supply stores. As well, you will require a large plastic or wooden spoon or paddle to stir the mash, and a floating dairy thermometer or a brewers' mashing thermometer in the range of 0-110°C (32-230°F). These can be purchased at homebrewing and winemaking supply shops.

The mash pot can easily be heated on any standard kitchen gas or electric stove burner. It's best to use the larger burners rather than the smaller burners, but both will work.

The Fermenters

For fermenting you will require at least three 30L (8 US gallon) food-grade plastic pails with lids. 30L pails hold 30L with 2 or 3 cm (an inch or so) to spare. Such pails can be obtained as empty bulk food containers from restaurants or health-food stores, or purchased quite cheaply at homebrewing and winemaking supply stores as specially designed fermenters with volume graduations on the side and with a hole in the lid for a fermentation lock. A fermentation lock is not really necessary for a grain-mash fermentation because there will be no extended or secondary fermentation done.

Ancillary Equipment

Siphon: You will need a 2M (6') piece of ½" vinyl siphon tube with a racking cane. A racking cane is a hard cane-shaped acrylic tube of a size that the ½" vinyl siphon tube will fit over. These can be purchased at any homebrewing and winemaking supply shop.

Refractometer: There are two kinds of refractometers that can be useful for home distilling: One is a refractometer for measuring the sugar content, or Specific Gravity (SG), of the mash; and the other is for determining the percent alcohol of the distillate emerging from the still. They are easy to use and can measure very small samples (ie. 3 drops) of liquid.

However, they are fairly expensive and can generally only be purchased from scientific suppliers. They're also of limited accuracy since there are numerous factors that can skew their readings.

Hydrometer: A standard winemaking hydrometer can be purchased at any homebrewing and winemaking supply shop. It's strongly recommended that you use a hydrometer rather than a refractometer, hydrometers are much more consistent and accurate.

Proof Hydrometer: A proof hydrometer is a hydrometer for measuring % alcohol content of a distilled spirit. A lot of homebrewing and winemaking supply shops carry them. They can also be purchased from scientific and laboratory suppliers.

For making whiskey it's very useful to have two proof hydrometers, one that graduated from 0 to 50% abv (alcohol by volume), and one that's graduated from 50 to 100% abv. The 50 to 100% one gives a more accurate measure of the begin- and end-cuts at 80 and 65% abv respectively. Most proof hydrometers that are graduated in those ranges are calibrated at 20°C, this is what you'll need to buy in order to use the *Proof-Hydrometer Correction Table* at *Appendix B*.

Hydrometer Cylinder: A 250mL graduated cylinder can be used for measuring SG with the winemaking hydrometer. It also makes an excellent receiver for the spirit still where the quantities of each phase need to be measured and recorded. Most homebrewing and winemaking shops carry hydrometer cylinders, but they are usually not graduated (ie. have markings on the side indicating the volume). Most people will have to go to a scientific supplier for a 250mL graduated cylinder. Also, make sure the cylinder is made of glass or some other alcohol-resistant material. A lot homebrewing and winemaking supply shops sell acrylic hydrometer cylinders. Acrylic is not acceptable for containing distilled spirits. Acrylic cylinders are okay for a wine or beer up to 10-20%, but for a 40-50% first run or a 90+% spirit-run they will dissolve.

Proof-Hydrometer Cylinder: For measuring the begin- and end-cuts of a small-scale whiskey run you'll need to be able to measure the percent alcohol of as small a sample as possible of distillate, and a 250mL cylinder would require a sample of about 200mL. This is much too large, so you will need a cylinder narrow enough to enable the measurement of samples as small as 50 or 70mL.

What you really need is a glass cylinder that has an inside diameter that's only about 1 to 3 mm larger than the diameter of the proof hydrometer. It's unlikely that you could find a cylinder with these exact dimensions to suit your hydrometer, so you'll need to get one specially made. This is not all that difficult or expensive. A very good way to get a narrow proof-hydrometer cylinder is to take the hydrometer to a university glassblower and ask him/her to take a 30 cm (12") piece of glass tubing that's 1 to 3 mm larger than the diameter of the hydrometer and put a glass base on it. Numerous people have done exactly this and the glassblowers typically charge about $5 for their trouble. As far as glassblower tasks go, this is a trivial job.

pH Meter: A pH meter is a device for measuring the pH of an aqueous solution (ie. the acidity or alkalinity of a solution in water). pH meters need to be calibrated from time to time to a specific pH using a special buffering solution of known pH. For mashing, the pH-meter precision should be calibrated to around pH 6 (say a buffering solution of pH 6.01). However, buffering solutions of pH 6.01 are hard to find, so you may have to settle for a pH 4.01.

Good pH meters are now available at a lot of homebrewing supply shops at a very affordable price and they are more than satisfactory for mashing. These will do just fine.

If you decide not to invest in a pH meter, pH papers will certainly suffice, but they are much more time consuming.

pH Papers: If you don't have a pH meter you will require two ranges of pH papers: pH 2-12; and pH 4.5-6.5.

Tincture of Iodine: Iodine is used to test for the completion of starch conversion during the mashing process, and thereby the end of the mash cycle. It's called the "iodine starch test".

The way it works is that when iodine is exposed to starch it instantly turns as blue as ink. So, at the beginning of the mashing process before all the starches are converted to sugars, a drop of iodine would instantly turn blue if it came into contact with a small sample of the mash. However, later in the mash cycle when all the starches have been converted to sugars, a drop of iodine would not turn blue, but would stay its usual brown colour. In fact, this ability of iodine to detect starch is very sensitive, even the smallest trace of starch will result in the iodine turning blue. So, when the iodine stays brown after contacting the small sample of mash, this indicates the conversion to sugars is very complete. More will be said about the iodine starch test in *Chapter 6 Mashing*.

The iodine used can simply be the tincture of iodine sold in pharmacies.

<u>Transfer Hoses</u>

Both the beer stripper and the spirit still (both described below) are filled, emptied, and flushed out using the upper and lower ball valves on the sides of their boilers. Generally, the lower ball valve is used for filling and draining and the upper is used for flushing. However, some setups may favour using the upper ball valve for filling as well.

To make the required transfer hoses, you will need:

Qty	Description
8-16M (25-50')	3/8" clear vinyl hose
4	female garden-hose couplings
5	½" hose clamps
1	siphon starter (alcohol resistant, eg. not made of acrylic)

Filler-hose: The filler-hose should be about 1.8M (6') long. It will need to reach to the lower ball valve on the boiler from the mash container, which must be placed at a height above the boiler.

Attach a female garden-hose coupling to one end of the filler-hose and secure it with a ½" hose clamp. Attach the siphon starter to the other end and secure it with a ½" hose clamp.

Drain-hose: The drain-hose will need to reach from the bottom ball valve to a floor drain.

Cut the drain-hose to length, attach a female garden-hose coupling to one end, and secure it with a ½" hose clamp. The other end is led to a floor drain.

Flushing-hose: The flushing-hose will need to reach from a faucet equipped with a garden-hose fitting to the upper ball valve. Almost all faucets can be equipped with a garden-hose fitting, it's typically done by unscrewing the aerator attachment that usually comes installed on faucets and screwing on a faucet-to-garden-hose adapter.

Cut the flushing-hose to length, attach a female garden-hose coupling to each end, and secure them with ½" hose clamps.

Immersion Chiller (Optional)

An immersion chiller is used to chill the mash down to fermentation temperature after the mashing process is complete. This will be explained in *Chapter 6 Mashing*. For the batch size discussed in this book (30L), the mash will cool to fermentation temperature in 8 to

10 hours. Leaving it overnight can easily accommodate this. But for larger quantities, it will require force cooling with an immersion chiller.

An immersion chiller is basically a coil of 3/8" copper tubing about 8M (25') long that is immersed in the hot mash with cold water flowing through the tubing. The immersion chiller described here will force cool a 30L (8 US gallons) batch of mash from 63°C (145°F) to 38°C (100°F) in about 10 minutes. It can be used to chill batch sizes up to 75L (20 US gallons) in about 30 minutes.

To make an immersion chiller, you will need:

Qty	Description
8M (25')	3/8" copper tubing
6M (20')	3/8" clear vinyl hose
1	female garden-hose coupling
1	faucet-to-garden-hose adapter
3	½" hose clamps
1.8M (6')	bare copper wire

Bend the 3/8" copper tubing into a coil about 25cm (10") in diameter. Usually, copper tubing comes coiled at about that diameter so this step will probably already be done for you.

Next, with the coil sitting on a flat surface with the coils running parallel to the surface, bend the two ends of the tube (one from the top, the other from the bottom of the coil) upward so that both stand roughly 50cm (20") from the surface. Place the coil in the mash pot and, at a point where they clear the top of the mash pot, bend the ends in smooth arcs until they are horizontal and side-by-side. Take care not to crimp the tubing.

Using a pair of needle-nose pliers wrap the bare copper wire around and between each coil in the chiller to brace the coil and hold its shape. Do this in four places around the coil. See Figure 1.

30   *Making Pure Corn Whiskey*

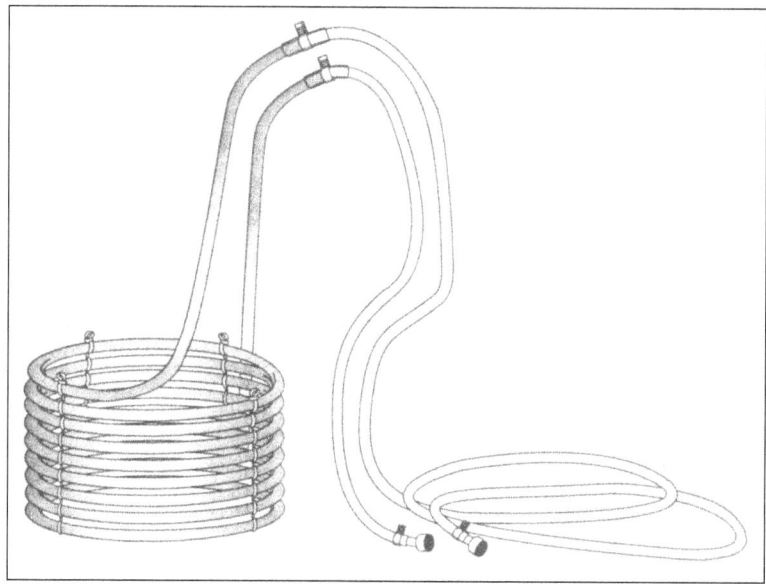

Figure 1

To hook up the cold water supply and drain hoses, cut two pieces of 3/8" vinyl hose, one to reach from the nearest water faucet to where the chiller will be employed, and one from the chiller to the drain. The supply hose should be connected to the end that leads to the bottom of the coil, and the drain hose to the other end. Attach the female garden-hose coupling to the other end of the supply hose. Secure all three connections with ½" hose clamps.

To connect the female garden-hose coupling to the water faucet, unscrew anything such as an aerator that would be attached to the faucet and screw the faucet-to-garden-hose adapter onto the faucet.

To use the immersion chiller, place the chiller in the mash about 10 minutes before you will be chilling. This will sterilize the chiller. Screw the chiller supply hose to the faucet and lead the drain hose to the sink or to a floor drain. Start the cold water running at a fairly brisk rate, and gently stir the mash while it's chilling. If you don't stir it will just take longer.

Monitor the temperature while it is chilling. When it's down to fermentation temperature, usually about 38°C (100°F), the cold water can be turned off and the chiller removed.

If you have a lawn that needs watering, the drain hose can be fitted with a male garden-hose coupling and a regular garden hose can be attached to the drain hose so the effluent water can be directed to a sprinkler or a nozzle. This way the spent chiller water can at least be put to use watering the lawn.

Spirit Still

The crude distillate (ie. low wines) from the beer-stripping runs is transferred to a fractional distillation apparatus called the "spirit still" as shown in Figure 2.

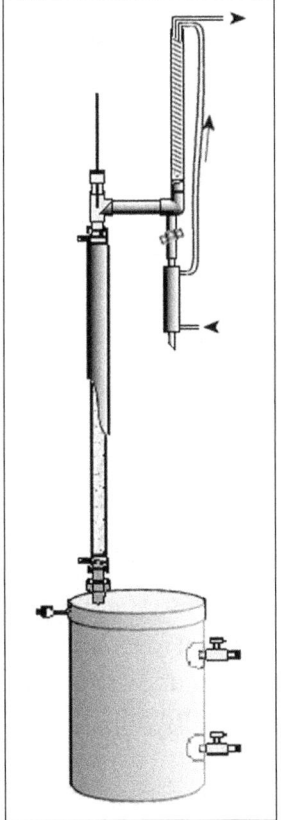

Figure 2

The fractional distillation apparatus described here is a high-separation still capable of producing pure alcohol, and would not normally be viewed as a spirit still appropriate for producing whiskey. However, as explained later in *Chapter 8 Distillation Principles and Practices*, the fractionating still can be operated in a manner that reduces the separation to a level suited to producing whiskey. This design was chosen in order to afford the amateur a more consistent and systematic mode of operation, unlike the precarious and temperamental operation of a more traditional whiskey still. Also, traditional whiskey stills are much more predisposed to yielding an excess of fusel alcohols into the distillate if they are inadvertently operated too hot or too late into the process. A fractionating still offers much more control over separation making it easier to guard against this.

Note: An excess of fusel alcohols (formerly called "fusel oils") does not create a poisonous condition in the whiskey, but it will make the whiskey taste base and grainy, and will cause the partaker to get a very bad hangover.

An obvious advantage to building a fractionating still to make whiskey is that the still can also be used to produce pure alcohol for making gin, vodka, and essence-based spirits.

Material of Construction: There are three materials that stills are commonly made from, and they are: glass; copper; and stainless steel. Glass is the most aesthetically pleasing, but not at all practical.

A glass still would be very expensive to make, could not typically be made by one's self at home, and would be very fragile.

Stainless steel is an excellent material for a still, but again is not one that an amateur will find easy to work with. Parts such as stainless steel tees are difficult to find and can mean the fabricator would have to do some cutting, shaping, and butt-welding. Also, stainless steel requires very skilled high-temperature welding. And, stainless steel parts are very expensive.

Copper is, by far, the most practical material for making stills. The parts are relatively inexpensive, and are readily available from any home building supply store or plumbing supply shop and, most importantly, it can be worked with and soldered together easily by amateurs.

Commercial whiskey distilleries have used copper stills for centuries so it is clearly a very acceptable metal to use. In fact, it's important that there be some copper in the construction of any still. Even if the still were made of glass or stainless steel, some components such as the packing should be made of copper. Fermentation produces small amounts of sulphides such as dimethyl sulphide, mercaptans, and hydrogen sulphide. Copper reacts instantly with these sulphides thereby removing them from the distillate. If a still were made with no copper, and sulphides persisted into the finished whiskey, the whiskey would have a rubbery, cooked cabbage smell and taste to it. Fortunately, sulphides will dissipate from the whiskey over a period of a few weeks. Anyway, this becomes one more reason to choose copper.

Construction: The following is a list of all the components required to build a fractionating spirit still. With the exception of the thermometer, all of these components can be purchased at home building supply stores and/or plumbing supply shops.

Qty	Description
	45L (12 US gallon) electric water heater
	3000W 240V water heater element
	¾" copper or brass male adapter (male thread to female sweat)
	¾" x 1¼" copper couplings
	1¼" copper union
7.5 cm (3")	¾" copper pipe
1.8M (6')	1¼" copper pipe
	1¼" copper tee
	1¼" copper elbow
25 cm (10")	3/8" copper tubing
	3/8" needle valve
15 cm (6")	½" copper pipe
2	½" copper pipe caps
8M (25')	3/16" copper tubing
2	¾" ball valves
2	¾" plumbing to garden-hose adapters
	1¼" copper pipe cap
	3/8" x ¼" compression coupling

	humidifier tap-valve kit (½" saddle valve and 8M (25') 3/16" plastic tubing)
	laboratory thermometer (0°-110° C (32° -230° F))
3	large copper scrubbers, or structured packing
	90° electrical box connector
	120V 3-prong plug
	heavy-duty extension cord
	grounded electrical timer
	lead-free solder kit
	Teflon tape
1.8M (6')	piece of 1 3/8" I.D. x ½"-wall Armaflex®
2	3" hose clamps
	adjustable shelf and mounting brackets

The various adapters and fittings used for the modifications are connected together by either threaded plumbing fittings or soldered sweat fittings. Teflon tape should be used on all threaded connections to ensure a watertight seal. Simply wrap the Teflon tape around the male threads two or three times before inserting the connector into the female fitting.

Most solder contains lead, an element known to be deadly poisonous. Only lead-free plumbing solder should be used for the soldered connections in a still.

As shown in Figure 2, the apparatus consists of a boiler with a 114 cm (45") reflux column made from 1¼" copper pipe. At the top of the column is the still head where the vapours rising from the boiler are condensed and split into two streams. The major stream flows back down the column while the remaining stream flows into the receiver. Let's look at each part of the still in more detail.

The Boiler: A very efficient and inexpensive still boiler can be made from a domestic electric water heater. A 45L (12 US gallon) size, very common for cottages or small apartments, is ideal and is usually heated by a single 1500W 120V immersion element.

A ¾" female pipe connector will be found on the top of the boiler by removing the sheet-metal cover and the fiberglass insulation from the top of the tank. This is where the magnesium rod (ie. the anode) used as an anticorrosion device is installed. Remove it since it is not needed in our application and we need the ¾" female connector for the installation of the reflux column.

The anode is usually torqued in very tightly, so the best way to remove it is to place a socket wrench (often 1 1/8") on the anode fitting and use a 1M (3') length of pipe to extend the socket drive. Secure the water heater firmly and use the pipe and socket wrench to turn the fitting in a counter-clockwise direction to loosen it. Once loosened, it will remove easily.

After the anode has been removed, replace the fiberglass insulation and the sheet-metal cover taking care to make sure the ¾" female plumbing connector is accessible after the sheet-metal cover is back on. With many water heaters the cover will have a pre-punched hole in it over the anode connector. If there isn't one, then a hole about 1¾" in diameter will have to be made in the cover over the anode connector. This can be done by punching a hole in the cover in the right place and then using a pair of sheet-metal shears to cut the hole to the right size.

Somewhere on the side of the tank is a ¾" female pipe connector where a pressure-release valve would normally be installed. For our purposes we will not be installing a pressure-release valve, so this connector will need to be plugged. Take the anode removed from the top fitting and unscrew the magnesium rod from the ¾" male plug fitting and discard the magnesium rod. The male plug fitting can then be screwed into the pressure-release valve connector to plug it.

To the two side connectors of the water heater for the cold-water-in and the hot-water-out (¾" male-threaded plumbing connectors) attach ¾" ball valves, and fit the ball valves with male garden-hose couplings.

The Thermostat: The thermostat, which controls the temperature of the water in the hot water heater, must be removed or bypassed. Since we wish to boil the mash and collect the vapours, a thermostat that switches off the current at a temperature well below the boiling point of water would obviously defeat our purpose. At first thought, disconnecting the thermostat may seem dangerous, and it would be if we had a closed system, but as can be seen from Figure 2 the top of the boiler is constantly open to the atmosphere via the heat exchanger so there can be no pressure build-up. It is no more dangerous therefore than a boiling kettle of water.

There is very little point in actually removing the thermostat unless it can be used somewhere else. It's easiest to just bypass it. After opening the thermostat access panel, you will see four wires connected to the thermostat. See Figure 3. Two wires are connected at the top, and two wires at the bottom. Simply take a screwdriver and undo the wires at the bottom and connect them each with their corresponding wires at the top (ie. left bottom with left top, and right bottom with right top).

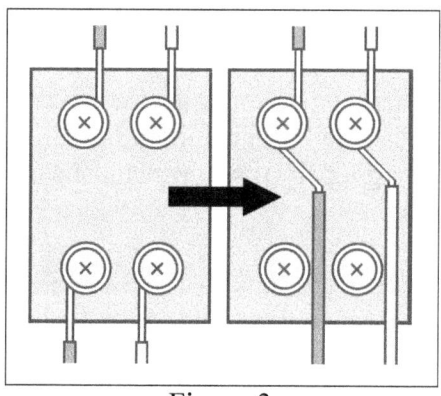

Figure 3

The Heating Element: The packed 1¼" column has only a limited capacity to allow vapours to rise up through the packing against the downward flow of condensed liquid (fractional distillation is explained in *Chapter 8 Distillation Principles And Practices*) so the boil-up rate must not be too great or the column will choke. The 1500W element usually supplied with a 45L (12 US gallon) water heater is, in fact, quite suitable for this still, but some distillers may wish to reduce it to 750W.

A simple and cheap way to do this is to substitute a 750W element for the 1500W one supplied. However, 750W elements are hard, if not impossible, to find nowadays, so an excellent way to accomplish this same end is to purchase a 3000W 240V element and run it on 120V. The current is cut in half, as is the voltage, so the wattage is reduced to one-quarter (ie. 3000 x ¼ = 750W). A bonus with this arrangement is that the current density in the element will be so much below its rated capacity that it should have a very extended life.

Also, a 750W element made from a 3000W 240V element has more than twice the surface area of a standard 1500W 120V element and produces only half the power output. This means that it runs considerably cooler than a 1500W element, which can guard against burning the mash. Sometimes if a mash has not been allowed to clear and has a lot of solids suspended in it, such as an excess of yeast slurry, it can burn against a 1500W element and give a burnt flavour and odour to the distillate. This is almost never a problem with a 750W element as described above. Of course, if the mash is reasonably clear this is rarely a problem even for the 1500W element.

Electric water heater elements are quite inexpensive and very easy to change, so it's wise to keep both wattages of element on hand, and use the 1500W element as the element of choice, but switch to the 750W element on the occasions when you are beer-stripping a mash that is very turbid and has not cleared well.

There will be a hole at the top or side of the sheet-metal cover of the hot-water tank where the wires to the 120V immersion element come out. Connect the wires to a 120V three-prong plug. The two wires to the 120V immersion element will be black and white, and there will be a green or bare ground wire. The three-prong plug has a round-shaped ground prong and two blade-shaped power prongs. One blade-shaped prong is wider than the other. Connect the white wire to the widest blade-shaped prong, and the black wire to the other blade-shaped prong. Connect the green or bare ground wire to the round-shaped prong. The wires are then secured to the sheet-metal cover using a 90° electrical box connector.

When running the still use a heavy-duty grounded extension cord to plug the still into a standard 120V wall socket.

Electrical Timer: A grounded electrical timer can be used at the wall socket to turn the still on (or off) at a prescribed time.

With a 750W element, a still with 20L or so of mash will take about 3½ hours to boil (and about 5½ hours with 38L). It's useful to have the still switch on automatically at, say 4:00 in the morning, and come to boil at 7:30. By 8:00 it will be equilibrating and ready to run off. This eliminates having to wait 3½ to 4 hours for boil-up and equilibration before beginning the run.

Of course, it's important to note that the heat-exchanger water will have to be running before boil-up, or the alcohol and congeners will not be condensed and therefore lost to the air. One way to mitigate this is to set the timer to shut off 15 minutes or so before it's expected to come to boil. The operator then attends to the still 20 or 30 minutes prior to expected boil-up and turns on the heat-exchanger water and disables the timer shutoff.

Another way is to simply turn the heat-exchanger water on at setup time and let it run all night. It's just a slow trickle. Perhaps you're not concerned about such a small loss.

A more creative way to address turning on the heat-exchanger water is to employ a 120V water solenoid. The water solenoid would be placed on the water supply tube to the heat exchanger and plugged into the same extension cord as the still. This way the heat-exchanger water would start running at the same time as the timer switched the still on.

A further refinement would be to attach a thermistor to the stillhead and set the thermistor to activate the water solenoid when the temperature of the stillhead exceeded a certain value. This way the heat-exchanger water wouldn't start running until the still actually began boiling.

Potentiometer: If you decide to employ the pot-still method of operation described in *Chapter 9 Distillation Methods*, you'll need to incorporate a potentiometer in the circuit supplying the power to the heating element, so that the heat to the boiler can be finely controlled.

A potentiometer is a variable voltage controller that can be used to vary the voltage to the heating element, thereby varying the amount of heat to the boiler.

Potentiometers, such as variacs as used in electronics laboratories, are very expensive and afford considerably more versatility than would be required for this application. An inexpensive potentiometer for this purpose is a household-lighting dimmer switch. Dimmer switches are quite inexpensive and offer very precise control over voltage.

However, it's very important to ensure that the dimmer switch chosen is rated for the power level of the heating element. Most standard dimmer switches as sold in hardware stores are rated for 600W. If the boiler has a 750W element, a 600W dimmer switch would burn out, so it would be necessary to choose a 1000W dimmer switch in this case. However, these are often not available in regular hardware stores, so it's best to buy these, and higher rated ones, at specialty lighting or electrical stores.

To connect the dimmer switch to the circuit supplying the power to the heating element, it should be configured outside the boiler and should be connected by plugs so it can be easily added and removed from the circuit by simply plugging the extension cord into it to include it, or unplugging the extension cord to by pass it.

It's best to install a standard surface-mounted electrical switch box on the wall near where the still is located and close to a wall socket. Wire the dimmer switch to the active line (ie. the black wire), as per the instructions supplied with the dimmer switch, and mount it inside the switch box and install the switch-box safety cover. Attach a plug to one of the pairs of wires coming out of the switch box, and attach a socket to the other pair. This way the dimmer switch can quickly and easily be included in or excluded from the circuit supplying the heating element.

Attaching The Reflux Column To The Boiler: To attach the column to the boiler, as shown in Figure 4, a series of adapters will be needed to go from the ¾" female pipe thread in the top of the boiler where the anode was, to the 1¼" copper pipe used for the reflux column. Connect a ¾" copper or brass male adapter (¾" male thread to ¾" female sweat) to the female pipe thread in the top of the tank.

Next, solder a 5 cm (2") piece of ¾" copper pipe to the sweat fitting of the adapter. Onto the piece of copper pipe, solder a ¾" x 1¼" copper coupling. Onto the copper coupling solder a 5 cm (2") piece of 1¼" copper pipe. Onto the piece of copper pipe solder the flare-and-nut end of a 1¼" copper union.

Solder a 114 cm (45") piece of 1¼" copper pipe into the male-thread end of the 1¼" copper union. The 114-cm (45") piece of 1¼" copper pipe (the reflux column) can now be connected to and disconnected from the boiler by means of the union.

It's useful to use some Teflon tape at the interface of the union to ensure a good watertight seal.

A 1¼" copper union is used in this set of adapters instead of a ¾" union in order to allow access to the packing in the 114-cm (45") reflux column.

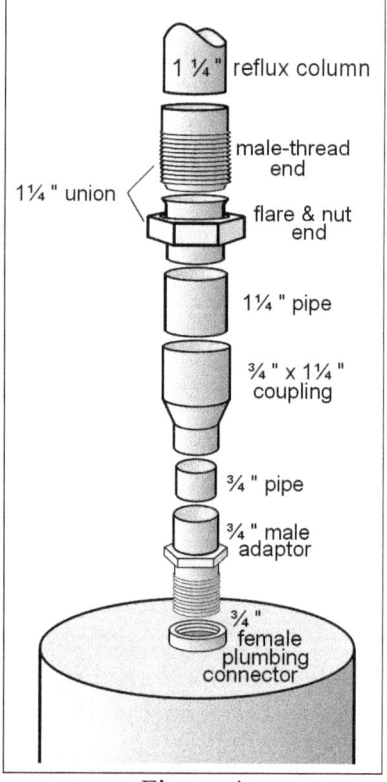

Figure 4

The Reflux Column: The fractionating column, or reflux column, consists of 114 cm (45") of 1¼" I.D. copper pipe. The bottom end of the column is joined to the top of the boiler by means of a union to permit disassembly when required.

At the top of the column a tee is provided for the passage of vapour across to the stillhead condenser and for a thermometer to measure the vapour temperature.

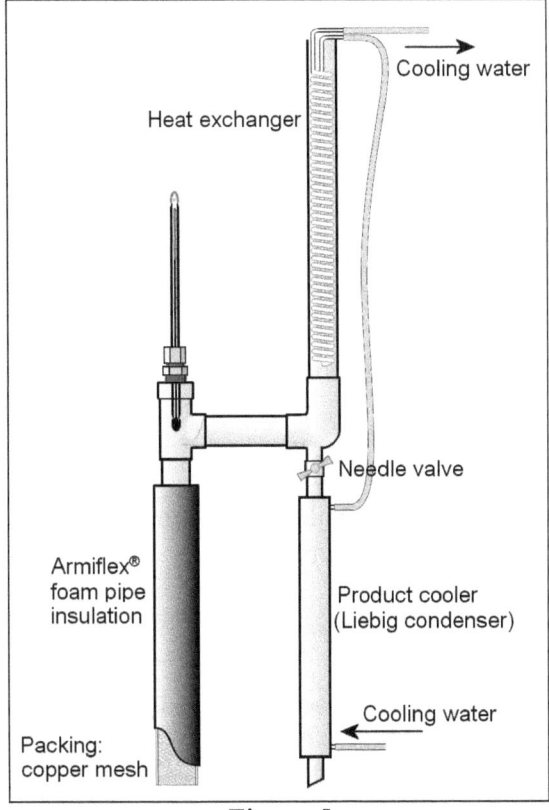

Figure 5

The column must be well insulated to ensure a stable temperature regimen within the column while it is refluxing. Use a 1 3/8" I.D. x ½"-wall closed-cell foam insulating sleeve, such as Armaflex®, as used in refrigeration and air conditioning systems. Cut it to length and secure it in place with 3" hose clamps at the top and bottom to prevent air from circulating between the insulation and the column.

The Stillhead: See Figure 5. The purpose of the stillhead is to condense the vapours emerging from the column into a liquid and divide the liquid into two streams. It condenses the vapour back to a liquid in the heat exchanger and, as the liquid runs back down towards the column, diverts a portion of it to the outside via a needle valve.

The stillhead is fabricated by soldering an 18 cm (7") piece of 1¼" pipe into the 1¼" tee at the top of the column to form the horizontal part of the stillhead. A valuable refinement is to have a tongue protruding into the middle of the column, as shown in Figure 5, to ensure the returning liquid cascades down the centre of the column.

To the horizontal part of the stillhead, solder a 1¼" copper elbow facing upward parallel to the column. To the other end of the elbow solder a 30 cm (12") piece of 1¼" copper pipe.

Solder a short length of 3/8" copper tubing, say 2 cm (3/4"), into a 3/8" hole drilled in the 1¼" copper elbow as shown in Figure 5. Attach a 3/8" needle valve with a compression fitting. This will avoid the necessity of having to heat the valve itself during soldering.

The hole for the 3/8" tube should be drilled in the elbow at a place where it will pass through both the elbow and the copper pipe. This will give the 3/8" tube a better purchase in the stillhead. Make sure the 3/8" tube is not inserted into the hole too far so as to dam up the condensed liquid and prevent the flow to the needle valve.

Liebig Condenser: The Liebig condenser is to chill the distillate that flows out of the stillhead through the needle valve, and to ensure that any vapour that may escape through the output tube is condensed to a liquid.

Take a 20 cm (8") piece of 3/8" tubing and make it as straight as possible. Take two ½" pipe caps and drill a 3/8" hole in the centre of each of them and make sure the 3/8" tube can pass through them. Take a 15 cm (6") piece of ½" copper pipe and drill two 3/16" holes in the side of it about 2.5 cm (1") from each end.

Place the two ½" pipe caps over each end of the 15 cm (6") piece of ½" copper pipe and slide the 20 cm (8") piece of 3/8" copper tubing through the copper pipe caps, and position it so there's and equal length of 3/8" copper tubing sticking out each end of the pipe caps. Solder the pipe caps to the 15 cm (6") piece of copper pipe first, then solder the 3/8" tubing into the holes of the pipe caps to seal around them. Finally, solder a 5 cm (2") piece of 3/16" copper tubing into each 3/16" hole in the 15 cm (6") piece of copper pipe.

This type of soldering where there are multiple solder joints very close together can be tricky in that there's a tendency to inadvertently melt one solder joint while heating the material to make another solder joint. With enough persistence and by cooling the material between each solder joint it can be done, but if you have access to silver-soldering equipment, what you can do is silver solder the pipe caps to the ½" copper pipe first, then regular solder the 3/8" tubing into place in the pipe caps, and finally regular solder the two pieces of 3/16" tubing into the holes in the ½" pipe.

Silver solder requires a considerably higher temperature to melt than regular plumbing solder, so once the pipe caps are silver soldered in place, the other solder joints can be made with regular solder without the concern of melting the silver-solder joints.

At this point, you now have a Liebig condenser, which is a 20 cm (8") piece of 3/8" copper tubing with a 15 cm (6") water-cooling jacket around the middle of it.

Insert one end of the Liebig condenser in the output of the needle valve as shown in Figure 5, and secure it in place using a compression fitting.

The Heat Exchanger: The condenser (heat exchanger) for cooling the vapour and returning it to the column is made from about 5M (16') of 3/16" copper tubing wound around a piece of ¾" pipe. It's best to start out with 7.6M (25') of tubing and wind the coils tight together until the condenser is 28 cm (11") or so long. Leave 30-60 cm (1 or 2') of tubing at each end to attach the cold-water supply and drain tubes. See Figure 5.

Wrapping the 3/16" copper tubing tightly around a ¾" pipe will produce a coil with an ideal diameter to fit inside a 1¼" copper pipe.

To dramatically improve the efficiency of the heat-exchanger coil some heat-sinking material should be loosely stuffed into the dead space inside the coil. Take a copper scrubber and untangle it and flatten it out. Using a pair of sheet-metal shears cut a strip of the mesh about 25 cm (10") long and 5 cm (2") wide. Carefully squeeze the mesh to narrow it slightly and gently insert it inside the coil so that it loosely fits the inside of the coil from top to bottom.

The top of the stillhead must be open to the air. A still has to be a completely open system with no build-up of pressure. The heat exchanger is inserted loosely into the top of the stillhead, suspended by its input and output tubes as shown in Figure 5.

As for supplying cold water to the heat exchanger, a standard forced-air furnace humidifier tap-valve kit can be used.

For a reflux condenser, the cold water should be input at the same end of the coil as where the hot vapours approach the coil. So, in the case of the spirit still, the cold water should enter the tube that leads to the bottom of the coil and be exhausted at the top of the coil.

For the flow-through Liebig condenser, the cold water should be input at the opposite end of the tube where the hot liquid/vapours approach the condenser. So, in this case the cold water should enter the bottom of the Liebig condenser and exit at the top.

The plastic tubing from the humidifier tap-valve kit should be set up to carry the cold water to the bottom tube of the Liebig condenser. One end of another piece of plastic tubing should be attached to the top tube of the Liebig condenser and the other attached to the tube that leads to the bottom of the heat-exchanger coil. Another piece of plastic tubing should connect to the tube that exits the top of the coil where it's then led to a drain.

The plastic tubing that comes with most humidifier tap-valve kits is the same diameter as the 3/16" copper tubing it's intended to fit over. This is actually a good thing, before trying to fit the plastic tubing over the copper tubing, soak the end of it in boiling water for a minute to soften it up. When fitting it over the copper tubing try and work it on a good 3½ to 5 cm (1½ to 2"). When it cools off it'll set very solidly in place over the copper tubing.

If the plastic tubing is of a larger diameter and fits easily over the copper tubing, then it'll have to be secured in place with hose clamps.

Heat exchangers of this design are remarkably efficient, and require a surprisingly slow trickle of cold water to thoroughly condense the vapours. When the still is boiling and in full operation the output water should not feel hotter than luke warm to the touch. If it's hotter, then the flow of cold water needs to be turned up slightly.

A thermometer in the stillhead measures the temperature of the vapour at the top of the column and is an excellent indicator of just when reflux has started. It's also useful for monitoring the progress of a whiskey distillation since the temperature constantly rises throughout the distillation run. However, determining the different phase transitions is much more subjective than simply taking a thermometer reading. This will be explained in detail in *Chapter 9 Distillation Methods*.

To mount the thermometer in the stillhead, drill a 3/8" hole in the middle of a 1¼" copper cap, and solder a 2.5 cm (1") piece of 3/8" copper tubing into the hole. The tubing should protrude into the hole about ½ cm (3/16"). See Figure 6.

Next, take a 3/8" x ¼" compression coupling and remove both compression nuts and both ferrules. Place the coupling in a vice with the ¼" end up. Looking through the coupling it

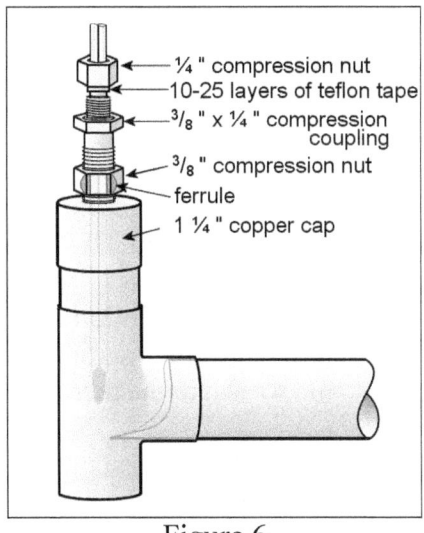

Figure 6

will be evident that the passage is too narrow for the thermometer to pass through it. Drill out the passage with a 17/64" drill bit. Try the thermometer in the passage. If it's still too narrow, either drill it out with a slightly larger drill bit or ream it out with the 17/64" bit until it fits. A slightly loose fit is no problem. The ¼" compression nut will need drilling out with the 17/64" bit as well.

Place the 3/8" compression nut and ferrule around the piece of 3/8" tubing that's soldered into the 1¼" cap and snug the compression coupling into place. Be very careful not to tighten too hard, the 3/8" tubing will collapse if the compression nut is tightened too much. Next, solder a 7 cm (2¾") piece of 1¼" copper pipe into the top of the 1¼" tee, then solder the 1¼" cap onto the piece of 1¼" pipe on top of the tee. See Figure 6.

At this point all the soldering will be finished, and the assembly will be covered with torch burns and excess solder flux, which will leave the assembly dirty and greasy. This can easily be cleaned up using an S.O.S. pad and lots of warm water, and should be done before the thermometer is installed. This will not only remove all the excess flux and clean up the torch burns, but it will also work very well to shine up the copper and the solder to leave the apparatus looking quite impressive.

After the assembly has been cleaned up, gauge the position of the thermometer bulb so it extends to the branch of the tee, but stays well above the tongue. It's important that the thermometer does not come into contact with the condensed liquid or the temperature reading will be incorrect.

To install the thermometer in the ¼" end of the compression coupling, discard the ¼" ferrule and wrap 10-25 layers of Teflon tape around the shaft of the thermometer where it meets the compression coupling. Use enough Teflon tape so that the thermometer fits snuggly into the ¼" compression nut. And finally, tighten the ¼" compression nut to secure the thermometer in place.

The overall height of the spirit still will be about 2.16M (7'1"-7'2") given that the 45L (12 US gallon) hot water heater is 56 cm (22") high. If height is at a premium, it helps to minimize the length of the copper tubes used as connectors for the plumbing adapters (see Figure 4) from the boiler to the column. Also, the 114-cm (45") column could be shorter if required. In fact, extensive experimentation has shown that this design of still will work very well with an reflux column as short as 66 cm (26").

Packing: The packing inside a fractionating column is very important, and many articles in the scientific literature have been devoted to the subject. What is needed are pieces of glass, ceramic, or metal which are inert to the liquid being refluxed and which have the following characteristics: they should not pack tightly, but should be of such a shape that they leave plenty of free space for vapour to rise up against a descending flow of liquid; and they should have a large surface area and crevices where liquid can be trapped.

For many years now home distillers and scientists have been using copper scrubbers, as found in the supermarkets and hardware stores for cleaning pots and pans, as packing for fractionating columns, and research has revealed that copper scrubbers are the very best packing that can be used for a column. It has also been determined that to optimize the efficacy of copper scrubbers as a packing, the copper mesh material should be organized in the column in a uniform pattern. As a result of this determination, scientific supply companies have developed a form of structured packing for laboratory applications based on the copper mesh used to make pot scrubbers. The structured packing comes in sheets of uniform mesh that are rolled up. Structured packing is now available to home distillers at a very reasonable price from home-distilling web sites.

To use the structured packing in the fractionating column, the sheet of mesh needs to be rolled loosely and cut to a diameter that fits snuggly in the column but still slides easily. Make a roll of structured packing as described and slide it up the column until it meets the tongue from the horizontal section of the stillhead. See Figure 6. You will need to use a broom handle to push it all the way up, but it's important that it slides easily and that the packing is not compressed. Make another roll and slide it up to meet the first one, and repeat this until the entire column is packed with structured packing. It may be necessary to trim the last one if it protrudes out the bottom of the column, but do not force any excess up the column to make it all fit, this would overly compress the packing.

If you don't have structured packing and will be using copper scrubbers you'll need to prepare them first to optimize their structure. Generally, you will need about three of the large ones that often come in packages of two. First remove the rubber band that holds it together in a wad and untangle it until it reveals its shape as a flat mesh forming a circle. Take a pair of sheet-metal shears and cut it to break the circle so the mesh can be laid out flat. Next, roll it gently along its long edge and cut it to a diameter that fits snuggly, but slides easily, in the column. Push it up the column with a broom handle until it meets the tongue from the horizontal section of the stillhead. Repeat this until the entire column is packed, and trim the last roll if it protrudes out the bottom of the column.

Note: There are cheap copper scrubbers on the market, typically available in discount stores, that are completely unsuitable as a column packing. These scrubbers are not actually made of copper, but of mild steel that's been painted with a copper-coloured paint. The paint will burn up and disintegrate in the presence of the hot alcohol vapour and leave the distillate with a pungent and sickening smell, and the mild steel will turn black.

These cheap scrubbers are easy to identify because they are not organized in any kind of a lattice of wire mesh, and the strands themselves look more like narrow ribbons of metal rather than wires.

Once the spirit still is set up and ready to operate, you will need a way to mount a receiver under the output of the Liebig condenser. One very good way to do this is to stand the still up against a wall (typically in the basement) with the horizontal section of the stillhead parallel to the wall. Mount an adjustable shelf on the wall behind the still, and adjust the shelf so as to place a receiver about 3 or 4 cm (1½-2") below the output from the Liebig condenser.

Filling and Draining the Spirit Still: The upper and lower ball valves on the boiler are used in conjunction with the transfer hoses described above. Typically, the lower ball valve is used to siphon the mash, or low wines (ie. output from the beer-stripping runs) into the spirit still, and to drain it.

To fill the spirit still, the container with the strained mash, or the low wines, is placed at a level higher than the boiler. The filler-hose is connected to the lower ball valve of the boiler and the siphon starter is placed in the mash container. The operator then opens the lower ball valve and, ensuring the top one is closed, operates the siphon starter to initiate the siphon from the mash container to the boiler.

When the transfer is complete, the lower ball valve is closed and the filler-hose is removed from the boiler. In order to ensure that the last of the liquid in the hose is transferred into the still, the operator can blow on the other end of the hose to force it into the boiler immediately before closing the lower ball valve.

It's important to note that if you are transferring low wines (40% or more alc/vol) the siphon starter must be made of alcohol resistant material. Acrylic is a common material for siphon starters these days, and is not alcohol resistant and must not be used with low wines. Acrylic will dissolve in alcohol and will contaminate the alcohol rendering it non-potable. This, of course, is not a problem when transferring an 8-10% alc/vol corn mash.

After a distillation is complete, the still can be drained by attaching the drain-hose to the lower ball valve. Lead the drain-hose to a drain and open the lower ball valve.

After the still has been drained, it can be flushed out by connecting the flushing-hose to the top ball valve and a faucet. With the bottom ball valve still connected to the drain-hose, and both valves wide open, the operator can flush water from the faucet through the boiler to rinse it out.

The upper side connector where the upper ball valve is connected is a ¾" pipe that leads into the centre of the water heater and bends upward and leads to within a cm (½") or so from the very top of the tank. This is because, as a water heater, the hot water must be drawn off the very top of the tank. In this application it serves very well to create a fountain effect inside the boiler that gives it a good rinsing all over inside when you're flushing it out.

Other Considerations: This type of still can be modified considerably from the design detailed above. If a higher throughput were required, the column could be made from 1½ or 2" copper pipe instead of 1¼" pipe. Since the maximum throughput rate of a column still is directly proportional to the cross-sectional area of the column, an increase from 1¼" to 2" is a 2.55 times increase.

The cross-sectional area is defined by πR^2. So, the cross-sectional area of a 1¼" copper pipe is $3.14159 \times (1.25/2)^2 = 1.23$ inches^2, and the cross-sectional area of a 2" copper pipe is 3.14159 x $(2/2)^2$ = 3.14 inches^2. Therefore, the ratio of the area of the 2" pipe to that of the 1¼" pipe is 3.14/1.23 = 2.55, so the maximum throughput rate of the 2" pipe is 2.55 times greater than that of the 1¼" pipe.

Of course, it follows that in order to exploit this increase in capacity it's necessary to increase the amount of heat supplied to the boiler by using higher wattage elements.

As mentioned earlier, the column can be quite a bit shorter than the overall 122 cm (48") detailed above. Experiments have proven that a column as short as 66 cm (26") will work very well. In fact, if the structured packing is installed optimally, it could very likely be even shorter and still work well.

The level of separation is a function of the ratio of the column length to the column diameter. So, making the column wider and/or shorter, reduces the level of separation. The above discussion about wider and shorter columns was based on retaining sufficient separation to produce pure alcohol. However, when making flavour-positive spirits such as whiskey, schnapps, or rum, high levels of separation are not required. So, if the distillation apparatus that you are making is strictly for making flavour-positive spirits and you won't be making pure alcohol at all, then even short/wider columns can be used.

Beer Stripper (Optional)

Beer stripping is a fast, crude primary distillation of the fermented mash in a high volume pot still in order to obtain most of the alcohol and the impurities in a smaller volume of water. This smaller volume, about a quarter of the original volume of the mash, is easier and cleaner to handle in the smaller precision equipment (ie. the spirit still) used for the final spirit-run.

The purpose of beer stripping in the production of whiskey is to afford a primary stage of refinement so as to enable the second distillation to achieve a suitable level of purity. It enables a comparatively large volume of mash to be quickly reduced to a much smaller volume that can then be refined to the finished whiskey in the smaller spirit still.

A beer stripper is really only required if you intend to maximize the throughput of your spirit still, where you produce a large batch of mash, then strip it in a beer stripper, and then finish it in the spirit still. This is more the sort of thing a commercial cottage distillery would do.

Most home distillers just use the spirit still to do their beer-stripping runs, and this is the recommended way to go unless you intend to run a little pilot distillery. The spirit still is actually large enough to accommodate exactly two 30L batches of corn mash. 30L of corn mash yields 20L of liquid to be beer stripped after straining. Two such batches would yield a total of 40L to be distilled. The spirit still has a capacity of 45L.

The spirit still is smaller and slower than a special-purpose beer stripper, but as an example of the beer-stripping performance that can reasonably be expected of the spirit still, as much as 300L of corn mash could be strained then stripped in five runs using the spirit still. The resulting 30 to 35L (8 to 9 US gallons) of low wines could be placed back in the spirit still along with a 5L (5 US Quart) adjunct of feints for a single spirit-run that would easily produce about 30L (8 US gallons) of 40% abv whiskey and about 10L (2½ US Gallons) of 60% abv feints.

If you do decide to build a special-purpose beer stripper, it should be a larger version of the spirit still. Use a large water heater for the boiler, say 113L (30 US gallon) or 150L (40 US gallon), and the column should be 2" or more in diameter. The column doesn't need to be as long, in fact, it can be as short as 40 or 50 cm (15 or 20 inches) since it doesn't need to achieve any significant level of separation.

The heating element should be 3000W 240V, and will move the distillate through the system quickly.

The larger water heaters often have two immersion elements, an upper and a lower. If there is a top element, it must be disconnected permanently because as used in this application the top element would not always be immersed and would burn out. If there is a top element that requires disconnecting, it's possible the lower element is only 1500W. If this is the case, it should be replaced with a

3000W one. A 3000W element should provide about 6L of distillate per hour.

The top element may be a 3000W element, so you may be able to switch it with the bottom element if it's only 1500W.

There will be a hole at the top or side of the sheet-metal cover of the hot-water tank where the wires to the 240V immersion element come out. Connect the wires to a 240V electric-clothes-drier cord. The drier cord will have four wires: black; red; white; and a green or bare ground wire. The two wires to the 240V immersion element will be black and red, and there will be a green or bare ground wire, but there will be no white wire. Connect the corresponding coloured wires of the element and the drier cord together using wire connectors, leaving the white wire on the drier cord free but covered by a wire connector or electrical tape. The drier cord is then secured to the sheet-metal cover using a 90° electrical box connector.

The beer stripper can now be plugged into a standard 240V electric-clothes-drier socket. If you are fortunate, the beer stripper will be located in a place near an electric drier and can take turns using its socket. If not, you will have to install a 240V service with a clothes-drier socket.

An electric-stove socket will also work, but it's different from a drier socket because a stove requires a higher-amperage circuit. If an electric-stove socket were handy, then wire the beer stripper with an electric-stove cord instead.

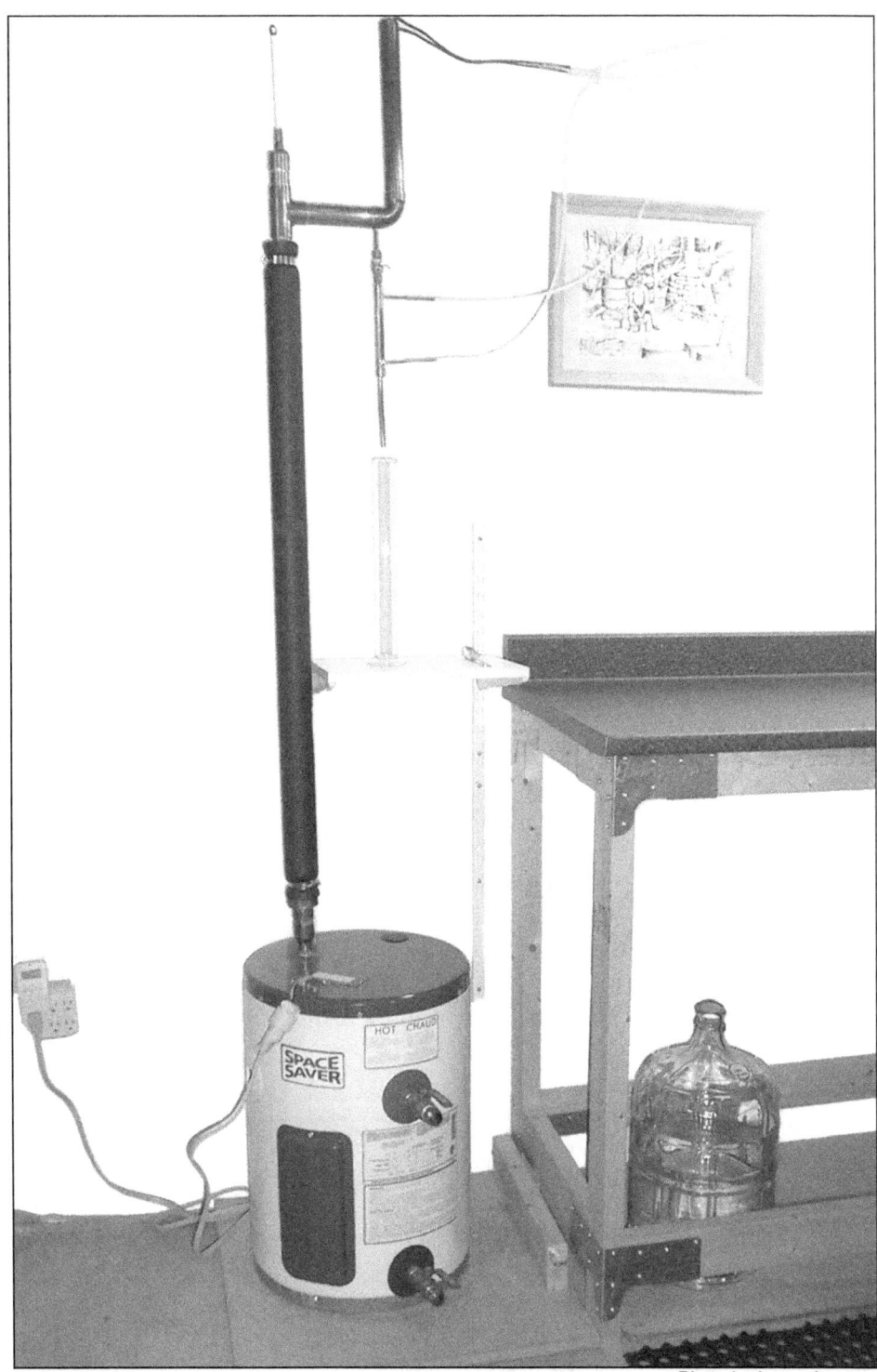

Photo by Lance Larson

Complete Spirit Still

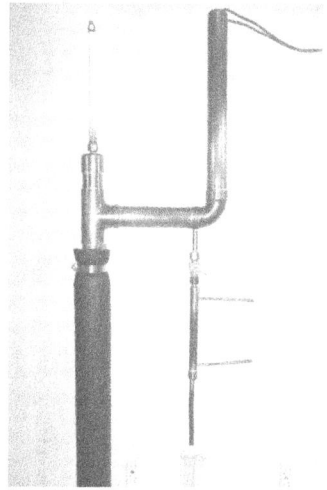

Still head

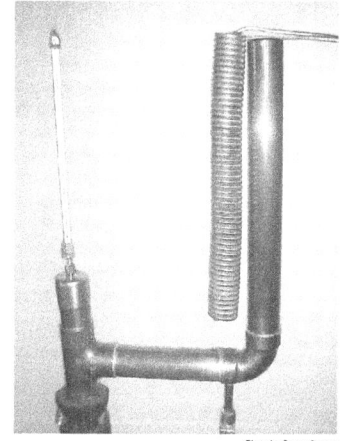

Still Head Heat Exchanger

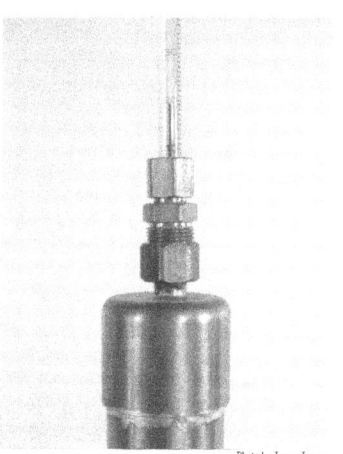

Thermometer Compression Coupling

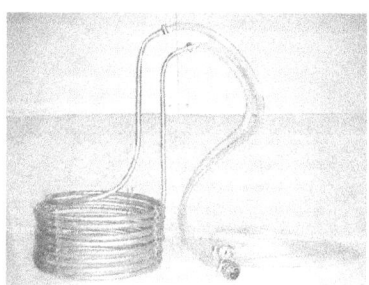

Immersion Chiller

CHAPTER 5

INGREDIENTS

Pure Corn whiskey is made from the simple and natural ingredients: corn; malt; water; and yeast. The mash should be composed of 80 to 90% corn with a 10 to 20% adjunct of malt to supply enzymes. Malt enzymes will be explained below and in *Chapter 6 Mashing*.

Corn

Corn in most of its forms (eg. cornmeal, corn flour, flaked maize) can be used to make whiskey. The corn should be top quality food-grade corn. The use of inferior grades of corn will typically result in inferior results. Some types of seed corn are treated with chemical fertilizer that would produce noxious off-flavours, and should be avoided.

The starches in hard grains such as cornmeal or corn flour require dispersing in the mash water by adding it to the mash water at near boiling temperatures and steeping for 10 or 15 minutes. This is described in *Chapter 15 Other Mashing Methods*. However, with flaked maize, which is already-dispersed corn that has been hot-rolled the way rolled oats are made, the grain starches readily disperse into the 65.5°C (150°F) mash water without the need of boiling or steeping at high temperatures.

Not having to introduce the grain to high-temperature mash water makes for a considerably more convenient mashing process, and for this reason flaked maize has been chosen as the type of corn in this text. How to mash other forms of corn as well as other types of grain is described in *Chapter 15 Other Mashing Methods*.

Flaked maize can be purchased at most health food or bulk food stores. Some such stores don't stock it because the demand for it for home use is fairly low, but most will gladly order it for you since it comes from the same distributors that supply all their other grain products. You may have to ask them to order it anyway even if they do carry it since you will generally want a 22.7Kg (50 lb) bag of it, which is often more than they will have on hand. Ordering it typically takes about a week. It can also be purchased at home brewers' supply shops.

At full retail price, flaked maize usually costs a little more than cornmeal, but if you buy a 22.7Kg (50 lb) bag it will be cheaper than the retail price of cornmeal.

Malt

The word "malt" describes a process, as much as it is the name of certain grain products.

Any type of grain can be malted. That is, sprouted then kiln dried to kill the sprouts. When grain is just beginning to sprout it produces many different enzymes to break down the endosperm (ie. the large starchy mass in each kernel of grain) to provide food to nourish the rapidly growing grain plant. The sprouts are heated in a kiln at this early stage to kill them and preserve both the enzymes and the endosperm before the young plants consume them. The malt can then be used as a source of enzymes to convert grain starches, including its own, to fermentable sugars in a beer or whiskey mash.

Of the many different enzymes produced during malting, the diastatic enzymes (ie. enzymes that convert starch to sugar) are the most important to mashing. Also of importance to mashing are the protein degrading enzymes. These produce nutrients that improve yeast performance in the subsequent fermentation step.

Most of the common grains (eg. corn, rye, barley, wheat) are available in malted form, but barley malt is by far the most widely used for making whiskey, and is therefore the choice in this text.

The best place to buy barley malt is from homebrew supply shops. These shops sell many varieties of barley malt, but only certain ones are suitable for making whiskey.

First of all, malt extract (available as syrup or powder) has no diastatic enzymes and cannot be used for mashing. Only certain varieties of all-grain barley malts have the diastatic enzymes needed to convert the comparatively large quantities of starches in a whiskey mash to sugar.

All-grain barley malts come in different varieties from pale malts to a full spectrum of caramelized and roasted malts. Only the pale-ale or light-lager malts stated to be of high diastatic power are suited to making whiskey. The caramelized and roasted malts have, for all practical purposes, no diastatic power. Fortunately, the above-mentioned pale-ale and light-lager malts are the main staples of all-grain brewing and are the most abundant varieties stocked by the homebrew shops. They are usually the least expensive varieties as well.

There are two types of high diastatic pale malts, two-row and six-row, and most home brewers' shops carry both. Six-row barley malt is well known to have the highest diastatic power. Six-row barley kernels are smaller than two-row because their endosperms are smaller. Even though the kernels are smaller, each kernel produces the same amount of enzymes as larger kernels. With smaller kernels there are more kernels per kilogram of malt, and therefore more enzymes per kilogram. However, this is no longer of concern. The well-modified high diastatic two-row pale malts made nowadays have very nearly the same diastatic power as the six-row malts and work just as well for making whiskey.

A lot of homebrew shops also carry wheat malt and rye malt among their malt selection. These malts tend to be of high diastatic power and are well suited to whiskey making. Their use will be discussed later in *Chapter 12 Other Whiskey-Mash Recipes*, but they can be substituted unit for unit for barley malt in any of the procedures described in the following chapters. After you are comfortable with the processes of whiskey making, it is worthwhile experimenting with different grain malts.

If barley malt is not readily available in your part of the world, it can be made at home from regular seed barley. See *Chapter 14 Making Your Own Malt* for complete instructions on how to do this.

One last word about malt is the crush. In order to mash with malted grains they have to be crushed with a grain grinder. Nearly all homebrew shops will crush the grain for you, or avail you of an on-premise grinder you can use to crush the malt you are buying.

Beer mash requires sparging (ie. a process of rinsing the sweet liquid from the spent grains after the starch conversion is complete). In order to sparge, the grain must form a filter bed that is loose enough to allow the liquid to pass through it. This requires a fairly coarse crush.

Whiskey mash doesn't require sparging so the crush can be much finer. A finer crush exposes slightly more of the enzymes and starch to the mash and is therefore beneficial. If the grain grinder is adjustable, adjust it for a fairly fine crush. If it's not adjustable, as a lot of roller mills aren't, the regular brewers' grind will work just fine.

Water

The Scots and the Irish have maintained for centuries that the secret to making good whiskey lies in the mash water used. Modern science has revealed that the characteristics of the mash water are not only important to the quality of the whiskey, but some (eg. iron content, and pH) are pivotal to the function of the malt enzymes.

The water used must be very nearly devoid of iron. A high iron content will denature (ie. destroy) the enzymes. On the other hand, a fairly high calcium content (50-250 Parts Per Million (ppm)) is beneficial to the subsequent fermentation and the resulting flavour of the finished whiskey.

Sulphates are preferable to carbonates or bicarbonates, but all are acceptable in the process. If you are adding calcium (explained in *Chapter 6 Mashing*) choose calcium sulphate (gypsum) over calcium carbonate (precipitated chalk).

pH: pH is a measure of the acidity or alkalinity of an aqueous solution (ie. a solution in water). A pH of 7 is exactly neutral, neither acid nor alkaline (eg. pure water). A pH below 7 is acidic, the lower the pH the stronger the acidity. A pH above 7 is alkaline, and the higher the pH the stronger the alkalinity. The full range of the pH scale is from 1 through 14.

Malt enzymes will function in a pH from as low as 4.6 to as high as 8.0. However, at the extremes the starch conversion will be very slow and incomplete. The optimum range is from 5.2 to 5.5, but conversion *does* work very well at 6.0 and even as high as 7.0.

Most source waters, even some of the best, will require *some* pH adjustment. This will be discussed in detail in *Chapter 6 Mashing*. Very few source waters are too acidic for mashing. Almost all are either close to neutral or are alkaline. Virtually all municipal tap waters are alkaline. Most have a pH between 8 and 9, but some are carefully adjusted to around pH 7.4. If a municipal tap water were even slightly acidic (eg. pH 6.9), over a period of years the water would corrode the metallic parts in the water distribution system. Because of this, municipal water treatment plants ensure the water is not acidic by passing the water over crushed limestone, which is a crude unrefined form of calcium oxide (CaO). CaO turns to calcium hydroxide ($Ca(OH)_2$) when mixed with water. This process is very cursory and does not offer very precise control over the resulting pH, so the resulting pH typically varies between 8 and 9. Some municipal water treatment plants use purified calcium hydroxide ($Ca(OH)_2$) instead of crushed limestone and adjust the pH to an exact value such as 7.4. Either way, the pH needs adjustment downward for mashing.

Most municipal water treatment plants will happily send you a copy of their current water analysis. All you really need to look at is: the overall hardness level; iron content; calcium content; and pH. Although hardness, in of itself, is not bad for mashing, it's generally preferable to have fairly soft water (ie. overall hardness level of 8 or less). Iron content should be very low, if not zero (ie. less than 25 ppm). A preferred calcium content is between 50 and 250 ppm, but if it's higher this is not a problem, and if it's lower gypsum can be added. The pH will invariably be too high, but this can be adjusted as discussed in *Chapter 6 Mashing*.

If suitable source water is not available, you can use deionized or distilled water as sold in pharmacies and supermarkets. It's advisable to add 10mL (2 tsp) of gypsum (calcium sulphate, $CaSO_4$) per 20L of pure water. This will establish a calcium content of about 150 ppm.

In the end, what we are doing here is emulating some variation of the mountain spring waters used to make the world's finest whiskies. Some of the more well-known regions are: the Scottish Highlands; Ireland; Kentucky; Tennessee; and many other areas in the Appalachian Mountains.

Yeast

Yeast is a living organism and is in the mould family of plant cells. The yeast employed to make any fermented beverage defines the character of that beverage. For example, a brewer can brew up a batch of wort and divide it into two or more fermentation lots. Each lot can be fermented with a different yeast strain along with its associated fermentation regimen to yield entirely different styles of beer. One lot could be a Helles-style lager while another could be a Kolch-style ale. Two very different types of beer and both made from exactly the same wort.

The same principle applies to whiskey. The strains of yeast used for fermenting grain mash are brewers' yeasts. But, the specific strains of yeast used by commercial whiskey distilleries are closely guarded proprietary secrets. And, each whiskey distillery seems to have its own strain.

The particular strains of brewers' yeast used to make whiskey produce an excellent ester profile and balance of character in the whiskey, and are known simply as "whiskey yeasts".

These whiskey yeasts are very attenuative (ie. they tend to produce a very low Terminating Gravity (TG), explained in *Chapter 7 Fermentation*), and as such are probably not found among the strains of pure yeast available for brewing beer. However, this is not to say that it isn't worthwhile experimenting with the pure brewers' yeasts, because each one does lend a unique character to the flavour of whiskey.

Bakers' yeast is actually a form of brewers' yeast as well, and since it's readily available and inexpensive, it has been used extensively by home distillers to make whiskey and other spirits. However, it's quite unsuitable for making whiskey. It produces a very unbalanced flavour with quite undesirable nuances, so it's strongly recommended that it be avoided for whiskey making.

Now, a homebrewer can go to a commercial brewery and most breweries will gladly give them a sample of their particular strain of brewers' yeast. But, a home distiller cannot seem to get a commercial whiskey distillery to share their proprietary yeast strain.

But, commercial whiskey yeasts have become available to home distillers recently. They are now available on the internet and at homebrew shops around the world, and some even come specially formulated for 25L batches of grain mash. In fact, one of the world's most renowned turbo yeast manufacturers, namely Gert Strand of Malmo Sweden, who is famous for his Prestige® Brand of home distilling products, has created a whiskey-yeast formulation for a 25L batch size that contains a full pitching rate of whiskey yeast plus a measure of amylo-glucosidase, an enzyme that will be discussed later in this chapter.

The author has done extensive experimentation with this whiskey-yeast formulation, and it yields positively excellent results. The flavour profile is excellent, and the yield is very high. It's also very easy to use, just open the package and add it like a turbo yeast. It contains the yeast and enzyme all in one.

This whiskey yeast is available on the internet at the following website: www.whiskeyyeast.com, and it's also available at many homebrew shops and home distilling web sites. It's more economical to buy at homebrew shops, so check there first.

Turbo Yeasts: Over the past 15 years or so, a series of yeast preparations for home distillers has been available called "turbo yeasts". Most of these turbo yeasts are absolutely excellent for producing pure alcohol for vodka, gin, and essence-based spirits. Turbo yeasts come in packages of 90 to 200gmand are typically formulated to ferment a 25L batch of straight sugar and water. They usually ferment 5 to 8Kg of sugar per batch and they produce from 13 to 20% alcohol depending on how much sugar they are designed to ferment. For the 13 to 14% formulations, they ferment in two to four days. For the higher alcohol contents like 17, 18, and 20%, they take up to two weeks.

Turbo yeasts are comprised of a high-alcohol-tolerant yeast strain mixed with yeast nutrients to supplement the nutrient-lacking sugar-and-water substrate they are designed to ferment.

These turbo yeasts have improved significantly every year since they were introduced, and it is anticipated that advancements in genetically engineered yeast strains will open the door to other dimensions of improvements.

However, grain-mash fermentation has little to gain from turbo yeasts. As mentioned above, turbo yeasts are formulated to ferment very high percentages of alcohol in very nutrient-deficient substrates. But, grain mashes are not nutrient deficient so they don't need the nutrients, and the high-alcohol-tolerant yeast strains are totally unsuitable for producing desirable whiskey flavours.

When choosing a yeast to make whiskey, try to find a whiskey, or at least a distillery, strain of yeast from a homebrew supplier or home distilling web site. The above-mentioned whiskey yeast from Gert Strand is definitely an excellent choice.

Alternatively, you can experiment with one of the pure brewers' yeast strains as produced for the homebrewing market by WhiteLabs®, Wyeast®, Brewers' Choice®, or YeastLabs®, and these are available at most homebrew shops. When using these yeasts for making whiskey, it's important to grow at least a 2L starter using sterilized wort to get the pitching rate best suited to a whiskey mash. In order to avoid adding too much foreign substrate to the mash, most of the 2L of liquid in the starter can be decanted from the yeast slurry before the slurry is added to the mash.

For any yeast you are buying you should always check the "use by" date. Expired yeast will not work for fermentation.

Glucoamylase

The term "glucoamylase" represents a family of laboratory-prepared enzymes such as amylo-glucosidase or alpha-galactosidase that are used in mashing to reduce, if not eliminate, the proportion of non-fermentable sugars in the mash. Mashing using malt enzymes produces a significant proportion of non-fermentable sugars (dextrins and polysaccharides). In brewing, these non-fermentable sugars are essential to the body and malt character of the beer, but in distilling they only represent lost alcohol yield. By employing glucoamylase, these non-fermentable sugars are converted to fermentable sugars and thereby increase the overall yield.

These enzymes as used by the distilling industry have not been readily available in small quantities to the home distiller, but some homebrew shops are now beginning to carry them. The whiskey yeast from Gert Strand is available in homebrew shops and it contains the required amount of amylo-glucosidase for a 25L batch of grain mash.

It's important to recognize the difference between distillery glucoamylase and the brewing enzyme, often called just "amylase", available in homebrew shops for making dry beer. This brewing amylase may improve the yield of a whiskey mash slightly, but it does not work very well in this capacity. Some home distillers say it makes no difference at all.

"Rhizozyme" is a form of glucoamylase enzyme derived from a fungus called "rhizopus oryzae", which infects the rice plant. Rhizozyme is well known in Japan as "koji", which is used to make sake (pronounced, sackee). Koji is available in some homebrew shops for brewing sake at home, and it's one of the best glucoamylase formulations for making whiskey. It has also become very popular with commercial distilleries as the glucoamylase enzyme of choice, and is available from the major alcohol-industry suppliers such as Alltech Inc, but only in large industrial-sized quantities. More will be said about rhizozyme in *Chapter 13 Traditional Sour-Mash Whiskey*.

One very good source of enzyme for whiskey mashes is Beano. Beano is formulated to prevent stomach gas from eating beans, vegetables, and whole grains, and it does this by helping the digestion convert non-fermentable sugars to fermentable ones early in the digestion process. Beano comes in tablet form and liquid form, and it's typically available in pharmacies and health-food stores.

For a 25L batch of grain mash, use either five drops of liquid Beano or three crushed Beano tablets. The liquid form seems to work better than the tablet form.

Beano works remarkably well, but it's not as effective as the proper distillery enzymes like amylo-glucosidase or rhizozyme, but if you have no ready source of distillery enzymes it makes a very good second choice.

It's important to know that all these enzyme preparations, including Beano, are heat labile (ie. they are destroyed by high heat), and should be added to the mash at yeast-pitching temperatures, and not at mashing temperatures.

Calcium Sulphate ($CaSO_4$)

Calcium sulphate, aka gypsum, is used to increase the calcium content of the mash water. This helps to prepare a mash water that emulates the properties of the mountain spring waters used to make the finest whiskies in the world.

Calcium sulphate can be purchased at home winemaking and homebrew supply shops or at chemical suppliers.

95% Sulphuric Acid (H_2SO_4)

95% sulphuric acid is used to adjust the pH of the mash water downward. This is covered in *Chapter 6 Mashing*. Only very small amounts, in the order of 10 to 15 drops per 20L, are ever used.

Sulphuric acid is an extremely dangerous and corrosive strong acid and should not, under any circumstances, come into contact with any part of the body or clothing. It should always be stored in a tightly closed container, out of the reach of children. Furthermore, it should only be handled by persons suitably schooled in laboratory procedures for handling strong acids.

If you are not comfortable with the idea of handling strong acids, then citric or tartaric acid (available at home winemaking supply shops) is perfectly harmless and not poisonous, and can be used with acceptable results. However, since they are weak acids, more will be required to achieve the same pH-lowering results.

If using sulphuric acid, it should be the common commercial grade available from chemical suppliers as 95% H_2SO_4, NOT battery acid as used in the automotive industry. Automotive battery acid contains depolarizing agents and other toxic compounds. Also, it's typically only about 5% H_2SO_4.

Calcium Carbonate ($CaCO_3$)

Calcium carbonate, aka precipitated chalk, is used to adjust the pH of the mash water upward. This is covered in *Chapter 6 Mashing*.

Calcium carbonate can be purchased at homebrew supply shops or at chemical suppliers.

CHAPTER 6

MASHING

There are two basic styles of mashing that will be discussed in this book: the "cooker-mash" style, which is detailed in this chapter as a modern, scientifically-optimized process used by commercial distilleries and adapted to home distilling; and, the traditional no-cook "sour-mash" style, which is detailed below in *Chapter 13 Traditional Sour-Mash Whiskey*.

PRINCIPLES

Mashing is the biochemical process where starches are converted to sugars. Starches are long chains of sugar (glucose) molecules connected by ether linkages. An ether linkage is where two sugar molecules join together and one water molecule is removed.

In mashing, enzymes cause water molecules to be reintroduced to the ether linkages, thereby breaking them and freeing the individual sugars from the chains. This process of breaking the ether linkages is called hydrolysis.

The term "starch" refers to a family of molecules, all of which are chains of sugars. Some starches are chains of as many as 400 sugar molecules, and others are chains of as few as four sugar molecules. Shorter-chain starches are soluble in water, longer-chain starches are insoluble in water.

The mashing process is comprised of two phases: liquefaction; and, saccharification. The liquefaction phase involves the action of alpha-amylase enzymes reducing the longer-chain insoluble starches to shorter-chain soluble starches, hence, "liquifying". The second phase, saccharification, involves the action of beta-amylase enzymes reducing the shorter-chain soluble starches to sugar molecules.

In the production of grain liquors, the starches are supplied by the grains being mashed (eg. corn, rye, millet, wheat, etc.). Grains are, for the most part, made up of starch, protein, and fiber. Although, different grains are comprised of slightly different proportions of starch, protein, and fiber, they are all roughly 50% starch. And, mashing acts on that 50% starch.

Malted grains (eg. corn malt, rye malt, barley malt) supply the enzymes used for the production of grain liquors. Barley malt is by far the most widely used, and is the choice in this text. There are laboratory enzyme preparations available for mashing, but they are most commonly used in very large-scale alcohol production. These laboratory enzymes will not be discussed here, with the exception of glucoamylase, discussed in *Chapter 5 Ingredients*.

For malt enzymes to work properly, there are certain optimum conditions that are important to observe. These conditions are as follows.

Mash Water: The water used must be very nearly devoid of iron. A high iron content will denature (ie. destroy) the enzymes. However, a fairly high calcium content (50-250 ppm) is beneficial to the subsequent fermentation and the resulting flavour of the finished whiskey.

Sulphates are preferable to carbonates and bicarbonates, but all are acceptable in the process.

If suitable source water is not available, you can use deionized or distilled water. The addition of 10mL (2-tsp) of gypsum (calcium sulphate, $CaSO_4$) per 20L is beneficial if using pure water.

pH: Unless you have an accurate pH meter, it's very difficult to measure the pH of the mash after the grain has been added. Most people use pH papers and, for all practical purposes, pH papers can only be used to measure the pH of the mash water before the grain is added.

Because the addition of the grain to the mash water will cause the pH of the mash water to go down slightly, combined with the fact that the conversion process itself results in a slight lowering of pH, it is best to establish a mash-water pH on the high side of optimum, say 5.8 or 6.0.

Measuring pH: To measure the pH of the mash water, thoroughly rinse a clean shot glass in the water to be measured. Draw off a small sample of the water in the shot glass, say 2mL. Cut a 1½ cm (3/4") strip of pH paper (of whichever range is required), and place it in the 2mL sample.

Allow the pH paper to steep in the water sample for a few minutes to enable the indicator to mix with the water and change colour. Hold the shot glass up to the light and compare the colour with the colour table on the pH-paper packaging and determine the pH of the water.

The pH papers in the range 2-12 are used to determine the pH of the untreated source water, and the pH papers in the range 4.5-6.5 are used to take the measurements of the mash water while it's being adjusted to 5.8 to 6.0.

Adjusting pH: A pH of 5.8 to 6.0 should be established for the mash water.

It is very rare that the pH of the source water is too low and requires adjusting upward. However, if this is necessary, calcium carbonate ($CaCO_3$), aka precipitated chalk, should be used to raise the pH. $CaCO_3$ should be used in comparatively small additions since a relatively small amount will raise the pH a surprisingly large amount.

As is the condition with most source waters, the pH will likely need to be reduced. Since sulphates are notionally more beneficial to mashing than other radicals, 95% sulphuric acid (H_2SO_4) should be used one drop at a time to lower the pH. As a general guideline, 20L of source water at pH 8.5 would take about 11 drops of 95% H_2SO_4 to reduce the pH to 5.8.

Warning: See *95% sulphuric acid* in *Chapter 5 Ingredients* for important information about safety and alternatives for sulphuric acid.

In order to avoid overshooting the target pH, it's useful to add the $CaCO_3$ or H_2SO_4 in small incremental additions, mix thoroughly, then take measurements with the pH papers in the range 4.5-6.5 after each addition until the target pH is achieved.

Temperature: The optimum temperature range for alpha-amylase enzymes (liquefying enzymes) is from 67°C to 71°C (152°F to 160°F). The optimum temperature range for beta-amylase enzymes (saccharifying enzymes) is from 60°C to 66°C (140°F to 151°F).

Since a temperature that favours alpha-amylase activity, 67-71°C (152-160°F), tends to produce a mash with a high proportion of non-fermentable sugars (ie. dextrins and polysaccharides), and tends to denature beta-amylase enzymes, it is best to hold to temperatures in the range that favours beta-amylase activity, 60°C–66°C (140-151°F). The alpha-amylase will work at the lower temperatures, just not as fast as it would in its optimum range.

If the mashing apparatus, or the mashing quantity, is capable of holding a single temperature constantly for 60 to 90 minutes then 63°C (145°F) is the optimum conversion temperature. In fact, many commercial whiskey distilleries use 63°C (145°F) as their conversion temperature.

On the other hand, if one is using a more rudimentary mashing apparatus, such as a large pot on a kitchen stove, then it is better to establish a conversion temperature of 65.5°C (150°F). During the 60 to 90 minute conversion rest, the temperature will slowly cool to about 60°C (140°F), thereby keeping the temperature within the optimum range throughout the conversion cycle.

It's important to note, that a mash at 71°C (160°F) or higher will rapidly denature the enzymes and may result in an incomplete conversion. Also, a large proportion of the resulting sugars would be non-fermentable. And as a final note, a mash temperature of 75.5°C (168°F) or higher will instantly denature the enzymes. In fact, heating a mash to 75.5°C (168°F) after conversion is complete is regularly done in the commercial brewing industry to "mash out" or halt all enzyme activity.

Iodine Starch Test: After the 90-minute conversion rest, the starches will be completely converted to sugars. This can be tested for by means of an iodine starch test.

After the conversion rest, there will be a clear light yellow liquid about 7 or 8 cm (3") deep on top of the mash. Using the floating thermometer, carefully dab a few drops of this clear yellow liquid on a white porcelain saucer or plate, taking care to avoid getting any of the mash solids suspended below the clear liquid in the sample.

Dab a drop or two of tincture of iodine into the sample on the porcelain saucer or plate. If there is any starch at all in the sample, the sample will turn an inky blue as soon as the iodine contacts it. If there is no starch, the sample will stay more or less the colour of the iodine.

You may observe tiny granular dots of blue in the sample when the iodine is added. This is not an indication of starch, but a result of cellulose from tiny particles of mash solids suspended in the sample. Iodine turns a dark blue, almost black, in the presence of cellulose in water. This is why you should take care to avoid getting the mash solids in the sample. Anyway, this cellulose indication can be ignored, and you can conclude there are no residual starches in the mash.

When the iodine starch test is complete discard the sample. Do not attempt to return it to the mash.

PROCEDURE

This section describes how to make 30L of corn mash (approximately 20L to be distilled after straining) in a large pot on a kitchen stove. This will yield approximately 2L of 45% abv corn whiskey plus about a litre of feints. It's recommended that you not attempt to scale this procedure up to a larger quantity until you have familiarized yourself with the process by mashing this smaller quantity two or three times.

A novice distiller may want to start out with the traditional no-cook sour-mash whiskey recipe detailed in *Chapter 13 Traditional Sour-Mash Whiskey*. The sour-mash recipe is much less exacting and doesn't demand the same level of attention to details like temperature regimen, and doesn't require any cooking or heating.

The reason the sour-mash recipe is not explained earlier in the text is it requires a knowledge of fermentation and beer-stripping so must occur later in the chronology of the chapters. Nevertheless, it's operationally more straightforward and easier to implement, it produces an excellent whiskey, and some novice distillers may find it a better starting point.

Equipment

>34-40L pot with lid
>a large plastic or wooden stirring spoon
>a floating dairy thermometer, graduated from 0°C to 110°C (32°F to 230°F)
>a pH meter, or pH papers – range 4.5 – 6.5 & 2 – 12
>tincture of iodine
>measuring spoons
>eye dropper

Ingredients

>23L of fairly soft municipal tap water. Eg. hardness level of 4; almost no iron; 100 ppm calcium; pH 8.5.
>10mL (2-tsp) Gypsum ($CaSO_4$)
>95% sulphuric acid (H_2SO_4); or, citric or tartaric acid
>8L (4Kg or 8.8 lbs) flaked maize
>1½ L (¾Kg or 1.65 lbs) crushed 2-row or 6-row pale barley malt

Method

This method is one of the simplest and least time consuming methods of mashing. Also, it scales up to large mashing quantities very well.

The principle behind this method, which is a single infusion-mash method, is to use flaked maize rather than undispersed hard grain such as corn meal. This eliminates the need to introduce the grain to the mash water at near boiling temperatures.

With flaked maize, which is already-dispersed corn that is hot-rolled the way rolled oats are made, the grain starches easily disperse into the 65.5°C (150°F) mash water.

See *Chapter 15 Other Mashing Methods* for procedures on how to mash other types of grain and hard cereal grains (ie. non-flaked grains).

Prepare the mash water by placing 23L of tap water in the large pot on the stove. Thoroughly mix the 10mL (2-tsp) of gypsum into the water, and measure the pH using the range 2-12 pH papers. Use this pH measurement to determine what pH adjustment the water requires.

Let's assume the pH, as with most municipal tap waters, is approximately 8 or 9. Begin adding 95% H_2SO_4 one drop at a time, mixing thoroughly, and measuring the pH with the range 5.0-6.5 pH papers between each drop until the target pH of 5.8 to 6.0 is achieved.

If citric or tartaric acid is used, which are both powders, the additions should be 1¼mL (¼ tsp), and will take about 10mL (2 tsp) or so in total to achieve pH 5.8 to 6.0 from a source water of pH 8.5.

If you accidentally overshoot the target pH with the acid, you can correct by simply making additions of 500mL of source water (ie. pH 8 or 9) and measuring the pH, until the target pH of 5.8 to 6.0 is achieved. Once this correction is complete, it will be necessary to remove a total equivalent volume of mash water as was added to do the correction and discard it, leaving 23L of mash water at the target pH.

Of course, if the pH of the source water were below the target, the water would require treating with calcium carbonate ($CaCO_3$) instead of H_2SO_4. Similarly, an accidental overshoot can be corrected the same way with additions of the source water.

After the mash water is prepared, turn the stove on high, cover the pot, and let the water heat up to the conversion strike temperature, 74°C (165°F). You will have to periodically stir the water thoroughly and measure the temperature as the water heats up until the strike temperature is reached.

When the water is at the strike temperature, turn off the heat, and stir in the 4Kg (8.8 lbs) of flaked maize. The temperature should come to rest at about 68°C (155°F) or higher. Stir the mash for about five minutes while the starches disperse (ie. gel into a thick porridge). It should take about 15 to 25 minutes for the temperature to cool to 66.5°C (152°F). The mash should be stirred every five minutes or so until it cools to that temperature. When the mash is at 66.5°C (152°F), stir in the ¾Kg (1.65 lbs) of crushed barley malt. Thoroughly mix the malt into the mash. The mash temperature should rest at 65°C (149°F).

Cover the mash pot and leave it for 90 minutes or longer for the starches to convert to sugars. It's helpful to stir the mash every 15 minutes or so during the 90-minute conversion rest.

After 90-minutes, the starches should be completely converted to sugars. This can be tested for by the iodine starch test described above.

After it's confirmed that the starch conversion is complete the mash can either be left for eight or ten hours (eg. overnight) to cool to fermentation temperature (ie. under 38°C (100°F)), or an immersion chiller can be used to force cool the mash to fermentation temperature.

At this point you will have 30L of corn mash ready for the fermentation stage.

CHAPTER 7

FERMENTATION

PRINCIPLES

Fermentation is the biochemical process where sugar ($C_6H_{12}O_6$) is converted to alcohol (C_2H_5OH) and carbon dioxide (CO_2). Yeast enzymes called zymase effect this process.

Yeast is a living organism and is in the mould family of plant cells. Yeast has two primary modes of metabolism: aerobic; and, anaerobic. "Aerobic" means in the presence of oxygen, and "anaerobic" means in the absence of oxygen. In it's aerobic state, yeast multiplies and increases its population within the fermentable substrate. In its anaerobic state, yeast stops multiplying and begins converting sugar to alcohol and carbon dioxide.

This transition from aerobic to anaerobic metabolism is a very natural process in fermentation. Anyone who has made homemade wine or beer observes this every time they add the yeast starter. First, the wine or beer goes through an eight to 20-hour lag time, and then the fermentation appears to start. During the lag time the yeast is consuming the dissolved oxygen in the substrate and is multiplying very rapidly. This is the aerobic phase. When the dissolved oxygen is completely consumed the, now abundant, yeast population begins producing alcohol and carbon dioxide. This is the anaerobic phase. The carbon dioxide is observed as the profuse bubbling that is characteristic of fermentation.

In order for yeast cells to be healthy and viable, the yeast needs certain nutrients, particularly, in the aerobic phase where cell multiplication is taking place. Among the many nutrients, nitrogen and amino acids are very important to yeast growth. Some fermentation methods, such as the fermentation of straight sugar and water, can avoid supplying nutrients by adding a very large charge of yeast. This avoids the need for an aerobic phase of cell multiplication because a sufficient population of yeast cells is present from the outset. However, the yeast has limits under these conditions. A straight sugar and water substrate with no yeast nutrients will rarely attain more than 8% alcohol before the yeast dies off.

In the case of fermenting grain mash or crushed grapes, adding yeast nutrients is definitely not required. Grain mashes and grape juice are bristling with nutrients, and ferment very fast and completely.

Grain Mash Fermentation

Grain mash, fresh out of the mash pot has a copious supply of fermentable sugars and yeast nutrients, but has very little, if any, dissolved oxygen for the aerobic phase of fermentation. This is a result of the long rests at high temperatures. You'll notice that boiled water tastes very different from water that hasn't been boiled. This is because the boiling drives off the dissolved oxygen.

On the small scale of 30L of corn mash, the mash can be thoroughly oxygenated by pouring it vigorously from one fermentation pail to another about four to six times. Also, vigorous stirring and rousing with a large spoon or paddle will work.

One fairly creative method of aeration is to use an aquarium pump to bubble air through an aeration stone immersed in the mash for about 30 minutes. This concept scales up very well to larger mashing operations. The idea being, to use larger pumps and aeration stones.

Fermentation Times

In the fermentation of wine and beer, the substrate undergoes primary and secondary fermentations. The primary fermentation is the vigorous fermentation that takes place over the first few days after the yeast is added. The secondary fermentation is the long slow fermentation that follows the primary fermentation. The primary fermentation only lasts a few days, but the secondary fermentation will slowly tick over for weeks, months in the case of wine fermentation.

A mash intended for distillation only undergoes a primary fermentation. Grain mash fermentations are typically 72-80 hours long, and then they are distilled. In fact, a secondary fermentation would be very deleterious to the ester profile of the mash and would ruin the finished whiskey.

During the primary fermentation the yeast is consuming readily available fermentable sugars. When the fermentable sugars have been exhausted, the yeast metabolism changes and begins breaking down non-fermentable sugars and other organic compounds and consumes them. This involves the secretion of very different enzymes such as permease that enable the consumption of non-fermentable sugars (dextrins and polysaccharides). This altered chemistry results in the formation of off-flavours that can best be avoided by using glucoamylase enzymes to ensure a minimum of non-fermentable sugars, and to avoid letting the mash languish too long after the vigorous primary fermentation has slowed down before distilling it. These off-flavours tend to resist separation by distillation.

As a general rule, a fermenting mash should be distilled as soon as the vigorous primary fermentation stops, or slows down to a spurious bubbling, regardless of how complete the fermentation is. So, unless the mash is still fermenting vigorously it should be distilled after no more than 96 hours after adding the yeast.

Specific Gravity (SG)

SG is the measure of the density of a given liquid relative to water. The SG of pure water is, by definition, 1.000. If a liquid were exactly twice as dense as water it would have a SG of 2.000.

For the most part, SG is used in mashing to determine the amount of sugar dissolved in the mash. Dissolved sugar increases the density of the mash. Water that is 1% sugar has a SG of 1.004, water that is 2% sugar has a SG of 1.008, and so on. Also, SG is used to determine the progress and the end point of fermentation. As the fermentation converts the sugar to alcohol and carbon dioxide, the SG of the mash decreases. It often decreases below 1.000 because the presence of the alcohol, SG .8, and the absence of the sugar render the mash less dense than water, SG 1.000.

When stating a SG, for example "1.065", it's pronounced "ten sixty-five" rather than "one point zero six five".

The originating specific gravity (OG) of a grain mash should be between 1.060 and 1.070. If the OG is very much higher than about 1.070, the alcohol content during fermentation will exceed 10%. As the alcohol content exceeds 10%, the yeast metabolism changes slightly, which can adversely affect the flavour profile. However, there are specific yeast strains that surmount this problem, such as the whiskey yeast produced by Gert Strand and other whiskey-yeast strains, mentioned in *Chapter 5 Ingredients*.

The 30L of corn mash described in *Chapter 6 Mashing* is formulated to yield an OG of about 1.065. If it turns out to be too high, it should be diluted with water until it's within the range 1.060-1.070. If it's too low, there's no problem. It will work just as well, except the yield will be slightly lower.

Measuring SG

There are two ways to measure SG. One is to use a refractometer. A refractometer is used by taking a few drops of the mash onto the slide of the refractometer, and looking through the eyepiece to observe the reading. Refractometers present their measurements on the Brix Balling scale. This scale is simply the percent sugar content of the sample. For example, a Brix of 16 means the sample is 16% sugar. The Brix scale maps to the SG scale by: Brix / 250 + 1 = SG. To go the other way: (SG-1) x 250 = Brix.

The main advantages to using a refractometer are: it only requires a very small sample; the sample does not require temperature correction; and, the measurement is not affected by the presence of mash solids suspended in the sample.

The other way to measure SG is by using a hydrometer. A standard winemaking hydrometer, available at home winemaking supply shops, is excellently suited for measuring mash SG. A hydrometer cylinder, also available at home winemaking supply shops, is used to collect a sample and float the hydrometer to take the reading.

The hydrometer works by floating in a sample of a liquid in the hydrometer cylinder. If the liquid is relatively dense, the hydrometer will float higher in the liquid. If the liquid is relatively less dense, the hydrometer will float lower in the liquid. The hydrometer has a scale along its stem, and the observer reads the scale just below the meniscus (ie. the surface tension) of the liquid level to determine the SG.

The density of liquids varies with temperature. Most hydrometers are calibrated at 15.56°C (60°F). This means that in order to get an accurate SG measurement, the sample must be at that temperature. Another way to get an accurate measurement is to measure the temperature of the sample, take the hydrometer reading, and then use the temperature-correction table at *Appendix A* to make the necessary temperature correction to the hydrometer reading.

For example, if a sample of mash were 33°C (90°F) and the hydrometer reading was 1.060, the temperature correction for 33°C (90°F) from the table at *Appendix A* is +.005. You would then add .005 to the hydrometer reading of 1.060 and get 1.065. This means the hydrometer reading of the sample at 15.56°C (60°F) would be 1.065, the correct SG of the sample.

To measure the Originating Gravity (OG) of a grain mash, it's important to collect a sample of the mash that's almost devoid of mash solids. When a mash has completed its conversion rest and has settled for a while, there's a clear light yellow liquid on top of the mash. A sample of this clear liquid can be carefully collected in a hydrometer cylinder and measured with a standard winemaking hydrometer.

Be sure to measure the temperature of this sample and use the temperature-correction table at *Appendix A* to correct the SG to 15.56°C (60°F), or you can chill the sample to 15.56°C (60°F) before taking the reading.

The Terminating Gravity (TG) can easily be measured with a refractometer, but cannot be accurately measured with a hydrometer until the fermentation is completely finished. This is because it's almost impossible to collect a clear sample of the mash that's devoid of mash solids until then. However, you can get along without an accurate TG, since all you really need to know is the change in SG over each twelve hour period or so. When the SG shows a very small, if any, change since the last reading then you can conclude the fermentation is finished.

Calculating Alcohol Content

When the fermentation is finished and you have strained the mash (to be discussed later), the strained mash can be left to settle for about 12 hours before it's transferred to the still. A fairly clear sample can then be collected from the surface and the TG can be measured with a hydrometer with reasonable accuracy. Remember to make the necessary temperature correction when taking the TG reading.

The alcohol content can then be calculated as follows:

For SG:
$$\frac{1000(OG - TG)}{7.4} = \% \text{ abv}$$

eg.
$$\frac{1000(1.065 - 1.002)}{7.4} = 8.5\% \text{ abv}$$

For Brix:
$$\frac{4(OB - TB)}{7.4} = \% \text{ abv}$$

eg.
$$\frac{4(17 - 1)}{7.4} = 8.65\% \text{ abv}$$

Also, most winemaking hydrometers have a potential-alcohol scale on them. By simply looking up the SG reading on the hydrometer that corresponds to the difference of the OG and TG (ie. OG-TG), you can rotate the hydrometer and read the alcohol content off the potential-alcohol scale.

Straining the Mash

After the fermentation (described below) is complete, usually 72-80 hours (avoid a fermentation time of more than 96 hours from when the yeast was added), the mash can then be strained and transferred to the still.

For the 30L of corn mash, it can be strained using a large nylon or cotton straining bag, available at homebrewing and winemaking supply shops. A 20L pail or 30L fermenter can be fitted with pieces of fine rope, like binder twine, so as to cradle a colander or straining basket near the top of the pail to support the straining bag. The straining bag is then opened up and placed in the colander or straining basket. The mash can be poured into the straining bag until it's full of mash solids. The straining bag can then be twisted closed and squeezed by hand. When most of the liquid has been wrung out of the mash solids, they can be discarded and the process repeated until the entire mash has been strained.

Approximately, 60% of the entire mash liquid will run off in the first pour into the straining bag. After the first pour and straining, the receiving pail may have become quite full and need transferring to another container.

Of course, this manual straining cannot be done on a large scale. For larger mashing operations there are specialized solids-separating machines designed specifically for grain-mash separation and they're available in varying sizes for small, medium, or large distilleries.

Also a pneumatic grape press used for winemaking works excellently. There are other forms of these grape presses, some are hydraulic, and others use an Archimedes' screw. They all work equally well, remove almost all the liquid, and operate on large volumes of mash very fast.

After the mash is strained, the spent grains are excellent fodder for any composter. The yeast benefits the composting activity. On the large scale, the spent grains can be dried in the sun (to eliminate the residual alcohol) and sold or given to a livestock farmer as a form of high-protein, high-fiber livestock feed. The spent grains are high in protein and fiber because most of the starches (originally 50% of the grain mass) have been completely removed by the mashing and fermentation, leaving behind only the protein and fiber.

PROCEDURE

This section describes how to ferment the 30L of corn mash produced in *Chapter 6 Mashing*.

Ingredients

>30L (8 US gallons) corn mash from *Chapter 6 Mashing*
>60gm(1/3 cup) active dried distillers' yeast plus 1 tsp distillery glucoamylase
>>Or
>1 package of whiskey yeast/enzyme combination

Equipment

>2 30L (8 US gallon) primary fermenters with at least one lid
>Or
>1 30L (8 US gallon) primary fermenter with lid, and an aquarium pump with an aeration stone
>1 standard winemaking hydrometer and cylinder
>Or
>1 Refractometer
>1 floating dairy thermometer graduated from 0-110°C (32-230°F)

Method

Initially, the mash will be in the pot on the stove with the lid on. The mash should have been left to settle for at least 90 minutes, possibly as long as overnight, and cooled to below 38°C (100°F). The mash solids will have settled out, and there should be 7 or 8 cm (3") of clear yellow liquid on top of the mash.

Measure the OG of the clear yellow liquid by using a refractometer or a hydrometer. If using a hydrometer, measure the temperature of the sample before measuring the SG and refer to the temperature-correction table at *Appendix A* to correct for the temperature, or chill the sample to 15.56°C (60°F) before measuring the SG.

The OG should be in the range 1.060-1.070. If it exceeds 1.070 and you are not using an authentic whiskey yeast (eg. say you're using a strain of brewers yeast), thoroughly stir the mash until it is mixed and take a hydrometer reading of the mixed mash. This can be done by simply floating the hydrometer in the mash and reading the SG. This avoids having to collect a sample in the cylinder. Also, no temperature correction is necessary for this measurement. This value will be markedly higher than the OG measured in the clear sample, and will not be an accurate SG measurement of the mash, but for this measurement we're only interested in the before and after difference. Now, make small additions of tap water, say 250mL (8½ oz) at a time, and mix it in thoroughly until the hydrometer reading has decreased by the amount the OG exceeded 1.070. The OG can now be updated by subtracting the amount it was reduced by the water additions.

For example, say the OG measured in the clear sample was 1.075. This would mean that the SG of the mash would need to come down .005. After mixing the mash thoroughly, the straight uncorrected hydrometer reading may be, say 1.080. Now, 250mL additions of water can be thoroughly stirred into the mash, and straight uncorrected readings taken until the reading has come down .005 points from the 1.080 (ie. to 1.075). The OG gravity can be updated to OG - .005 = new OG (ie. 1.075 - .005 = 1.070).

The mash produced in *Chapter 6 Mashing* is not likely to require such a correction if the quantities were adhered to.

Next, the mash needs to be transferred to a clean 30L fermenter. The temperature should have cooled to below 38°C (100°F) before it is transferred. For the 30L batch, the mash can be left to cool until the temperature is below 38°C (100°F). For larger batch sizes, it will be necessary to employ an immersion chiller to force cool the mash.

Once the mash has cooled to below 38°C (100°F) it can be transferred. This can be done by pouring the mash from the mash pot to a clean 30L fermenter. If the full mash pot is too heavy or too awkward to pick up and pour, the mash can be ladled with a one or two litre measuring cup into the fermenter until the volume is down to a manageable level.

For larger batch sizes, a grain pump can be used to make all transfers. Grain pumps are like sewage pumps in that they are capable of pumping liquids that are full of suspended solids. Some brewing operations use sewage pumps (new ones, never used for sewage) for making such transfers. Also, sewage pumps are sometimes used for Recirculating Infusion Mash Systems (RIMS) that constantly circulate a mash during the mashing cycle. This maintains a uniform temperature and provides the stirring function for large-scale mashing.

The mash is now ready for aerating (ie. providing dissolved oxygen). For the 30L batch, you can vigorously pour the mash from one fermenter to another four to six times. This works extremely well. You can also use an aquarium pump to pump air through an aeration stone placed in the mash. The aeration stone should be left to bubble in the mash for about 30 minutes. The yeast and enzyme can be added while the aeration stone is still bubbling in the mash.

On the larger scale, bubbling through an aeration stone can be used, perhaps using a larger pump and larger stone. Also, mechanically rousing the mash in a manner that causes splashing for 20 or 30 minutes will work as well.

If the mashing apparatus is equipped with a RIMS, as discussed above, the RIMS can be set up so that the output splashes into the mash. Fifteen to 30 minutes of such splashing would thoroughly aerate the mash.

After the mash has been aerated, the yeast can be pitched (ie. added to the mash). Place the fermenter where it's going to sit undisturbed for the next three days, and make sure the ambient temperature is between 21 and 33°C (70 and 90°F).

Making sure the present mash temperature is below 38°C (100°F), add the yeast and enzyme and stir. After 30 minutes the yeast will have hydrated in the liquid and can be thoroughly stirred in.

Within 60 minutes of pitching the yeast, vigorous fermentation will be evident (ie. vigorous bubbling). The bubbling will continually rouse the mash throughout the fermentation, ensuring the mash stays thoroughly mixed. Leave the mash for 72 hours from when the yeast was pitched. It's helpful to stir the mash thoroughly every 24 hours, but not necessary.

After 72 hours the fermentation will either be complete and the activity will have diminished to a slow spurious bubbling, or the fermentation will still be active and only have slowed down slightly. If the latter is the case, monitor it every six hours or so until the fermentation is very slow and therefore, finished. Fermentation shouldn't take more than 84 hours.

When the fermentation is complete, it's important that the mash be strained, and at least placed in the still, and heated to above 52°C (125°F) within 24 hours or off flavours may develop. This will sterilize the mash and prevent all yeast and/or bacterial activity from further metabolizing the mash.

When the fermentation is complete the mash is ready to be strained. For the 30L of corn mash, it can be strained by hand using a straining bag as described above. Larger volumes will require a mechanical device such as solids-separator or a pneumatic winepress, also described above.

After straining, the volume of liquid retrieved will be about 70% of the entire-mash volume. If the mash were mechanically pressed, the volume of liquid retrieved is closer to 80% of the entire-mash volume. In the case of the 30L of corn mash strained by hand, between 20 and 22L of liquid will be retrieved.

After the mash is strained and has settled for 30 to 60 minutes, a fairly clear sample of the mash liquid can be collected from the surface, and the Terminating Gravity (TG) can be measured.

With the OG and the TG, the alcohol percentage can be calculated using the formula:
$$\frac{1000(OG - TG)}{7.4} = \% \text{ abv}$$
In most cases the strained mash will need to settle for 12 to 24 hours to let the suspended solids settle out so only the clear liquid can be siphoned off and transferred to the still. Too much sediment suspended in the mash can burn against the heating element in the still. After the completion of this fermentation step, you will have about 20L of fermented and strained corn mash at about 8.5% abv, and you will be ready to proceed to the beer-stripping step.

CHAPTER 8

DISTILLATION PRINCIPLES AND PRACTICES

PRINCIPLES

Distillation is a physical process where compounds are separated by virtue of their different boiling points. If two compounds occurred together that had the same boiling point, they would not be separable by distillation. Fortunately, very few compounds have common boiling points with other compounds.

The separation in distillation occurs when a mixture of compounds in the still is brought to boil. Compounds with lower boiling points vaporize at lower temperatures than compounds with higher boiling points. This means that the vapour, or steam, rising off the boiling mixture has a more copious amount of the lower-boiling-point compounds than of the higher-boiling-point compounds. Next, this vapour is collected and cooled to condense it back into a liquid. The resulting liquid, called the distillate, contains a considerably higher concentration of the lower-boiling-point compounds than of the higher-boiling-point ones.

In a simplified example, assume a mixture of 90% water and 10% ethanol is to be separated by distillation. Water has a boiling point of 100°C (212°F) and ethanol has a boiling point of 78.4°C (173.1°F). The ethanol will boil and vaporize well before the water, so when the vapours are collected and condensed, the resulting distillate will have a very high concentration of ethanol and comparatively little water. Of course, the distillate will not be pure ethanol because some water will vaporize at the boiling point of ethanol, even if the water itself is not at its boiling point.

Because all the compounds in a still will vaporize to a greater or lesser extent during boiling, the separation of the compounds will not be perfect, so more elaborate stills have been developed to intensify the separation of the vapours once they have left the boiler.

In modern high-separation stills this is done by employing a reflux column to manage the vapours after they leave the boiler and before they are drawn from the still.

There are many different designs of stills. The most basic and rudimentary design is a "pot still" such as a closed pot, like a pressure cooker, with a pipe leading from the lid into a condenser coil. The condenser coil can either be long enough to air cool the vapours or it can be shorter and immersed in a water jacket. Such a still would afford minimum separation since there is almost no separation of the vapours once they leave the boiler. Although this design of still is not suitable for producing beverage alcohol by modern standards, it will still concentrate an 8 or 10% alcohol mash to 60% in a fairly fast run.

The next level of still is the "whiskey still", sometimes called a "gooseneck" still. This design has been in use for centuries for commercial whiskey production, and is just as popular today in modern whiskey distilleries as it has ever been. A whiskey still has a large boiler with a long broad neck rising from it. The neck bends at the top and leads to a condenser coil immersed in water. This design is very similar to the pot still design, except the tall broad neck affords enough separation to hold back most of the fusel alcohols from the distillate. This design of still is sufficient for the production of whiskey, brandy, and rum, for which it is very widely used commercially. The whiskey still is not suitable, however, for the production of vodka or gin, which requires a high-separation still capable of producing pure alcohol.

This brings us to the high-separation still design called a "column still" or a "fractionating still". A fractionating still is used to produce pure alcohol by fractional distillation for vodka and gin, or for pharmaceutical and laboratory use. The fractionating still has already been described to some extent in *Chapter 4 Equipment*. It will be useful to refer back to the diagrams and pictures in that chapter as you read on.

In a fractionating still the vapours emerging from the boiling mixture pass up a column packed with small pieces of glass, ceramic, stainless steel, copper or other material, inert to the process. In larger fractionating stills, the columns have baffle plates with holes in them instead of packing material. Each piece of packing, or the baffle plates, can hold a small amount of liquid, either internally (if they have internal crevices) or in the interstices between adjacent particles. At the top of the column the emerging vapour is condensed into a liquid by means of cold water running through a heat exchanger. The condensed liquid runs back down the column until it reaches the boiler where it is reheated, converted into vapour once more, and once again moves up the column.

At equilibrium, which may take several hours to achieve in the case of pure-alcohol production, the system consists of vapour rising up the column meeting a flow of liquid running down the column. At each vapour-liquid interface on the packing material within the column, a partial separation occurs wherein the more volatile components of the mixture go into the vapour phase and rise to the top while the less volatile components go into the liquid phase and are carried down into the boiler. At equilibrium, the many components in the mixture become stacked up in the column in the order of their boiling points, the most volatile at the top and the least volatile at the bottom.

In commercial operations that use a continuous-run design of fractionating still, the fermented mash is fed into the boiler from a reservoir, the different components of the mixture are drawn off at various heights along the column, and the spent residue is drained off. This process can continue indefinitely as long as fermented mash is fed into the boiler. Acetone, for example, would be continuously drawn off from the top of the column while ethanol would be continuously drawn off from a point a little further down.

Very small operations such as we are concerned with here do not employ a continuous-run system. Rather, fractional distillation is carried out batchwise. After column equilibrium is established, with acetone and methanol at the top and fusel alcohols at the bottom we start to progressively draw off liquid from the top of the column. First come the acetone and then the methanol and all the other low-boiling-point compounds. Then the ethanol starts to appear, and when it does, a small percentage of it is drawn off, and the remainder is allowed to run back down the column to continue the counter-current flow and the separation process. Eventually, the ethanol will be exhausted and the higher alcohols, the so-called fusel alcohols, will start to emerge. At this point (or in practice somewhat before) the boiler is switched off.

Water is an important constituent of the fermentation substrate and, with a boiling point of 100°C (212°F), lies intermediate between the least and most volatile components of the mixture. It has one important difference from the other components, however, in that it forms an azeotrope with ethanol. An azeotrope is a mixture of two liquids with a boiling point different from either constituent. In the case of ethanol and water, the azeotrope occurs at a mixture of 96.5% ethanol and 3.5% water, and has a boiling point of 78.15°C (172.67°F), .25°C lower than the 78.4°C (173.12°F) of pure ethanol. As far as a distillation system is concerned this azeotrope is a single compound with a boiling point of 78.15°C (172.67°F) and proceeds to separate it on that basis. The ethanol which is purified by a fractionating column is not, therefore, pure 100% ethanol but pure 96.5%, the "impurity" being pure water. No amount of redistillation under the conditions we are using will influence this percentage. 96.5% alc/vol is the theoretical maximum purity that can be derived by the above process.

If it is absolutely essential to remove all the water, for example if it is to be mixed with gasoline to produce gasohol, then special methods are available to accomplish this. For our purposes, however, where we are going to dilute the alcohol with water to 40 or 50% anyway, the presence of 3.5% water is of no consequence.

The high level of separation of a fractionating still is a function of the reflux taking place by the condensed liquid flowing down the column interfacing with the vapours rising up the column. When distillate is drawn off the still at the top of the column it is important that only about 10% is drawn off and about 90% is allowed to return down the column to maintain the reflux, and hence the high separation.

If the operator of a fractionating still wanted to reduce the level of separation afforded by the still, they could do so by drawing off a greater proportion of the distillate leaving less reflux, say 30% drawn off and 70% reflux. Or, even 90% drawn off and 10% reflux. This means that a high-separation fractionating still offers very precise control over separation level by means of adjusting its proportion of reflux. Thereby, making it possible to produce spirits that require much less separation, such as whiskey, in a fractionating still. And, it is because of this precise control over separation level that the author has chosen a fractionating still in this text as the design for making whiskey.

Whiskey Distillation: In the production of pure alcohol, a high-separation still is employed to separate out most of the water and all of the congeners (ie. impurities) and deliver only the alcohol. But in the production of whiskey, certain proportions of the congeners need to be left in the distillate. So, only moderate separation can occur. For this reason, whiskey is usually made in gooseneck stills that give comparatively low separation. However, some modern whiskey distilleries use variations of fractionating stills to maintain better control over the process.

Whiskey is distilled in two runs: a primary distillation, or beer-stripping run; and, a spirit-run. The beer-stripping run is generally done in a very crude high-volume pot still called a "beer stripper". The beer stripper is used to distil the fermented mash and concentrate the alcohol and all the impurities into a distillate of about 40 to 50% alcohol, called "low wines". The spirit-run is done in a whiskey still, either a gooseneck or a special-purpose fractionating still, called a "spirit still". The spirit still is used to distil the low wines and refine them into the finished spirit. There are actually two outputs retained from the spirit-run: the finished spirit; and, the feints (explained below).

To produce the finished whiskey, the spirit still is filled with the low wines from the beer-stripping run plus a measure of feints from previous spirit-runs. The spirit still is then heated up and brought to boil.

The distillate from a spirit-run comes out in four phases: the foreshots; the heads; the middle-run; and, the tails. There is another phase that will be mentioned, namely the "equilibration phase". The equilibration phase has no role in the distilling of whiskey but it's the condition that occurs when a fractionating still's output valve is closed and the still is undergoing total reflux condensation. Equilibration is important when making pure alcohol where it's necessary to give the fractionating still time for all the composite vapours to separate out in the column before the distillate can be drawn off.

Foreshots: The foreshots are the low-boiling-point compounds that come out of the still first. They contain acetone, methanol, various esters and aldehydes, and other volatiles. Foreshots are to be considered poisonous and should be discarded.

However, when the still is operated to produce whiskey (described later) where no equilibration is done there is no practical division between the foreshots and the heads so they are simply merged into the heads phase.

Heads: The heads come out after the foreshots, and have a very high concentration of alcohol. They are also laden with the bulk of the flavour congeners. The heads are retained and later mixed with the tails to make up the feints that are recycled through future spirit-runs.

Middle-run: The middle-run is the whiskey, and is the phase that runs between the heads and the tails. The entire middle-run must be collected in a single container and thoroughly mixed since its make-up varies from beginning to end.

The middle-run is best quantified as the cut that runs from the still from when the emerging distillate is 80% abv down to when it's 65%.

Tails: At some point late in the middle-run (ie. when the emerging distillate is between 60 and 65% abv) the flavour of the emerging distillate starts to lose its sweetness and takes on an undesirable harshness. This flavour is often described as thin, watery, grainy, and bitter. This is the point when the distiller switches to the tails phase.

The tails don't contain much in the way of desirable congeners, but they are typically run until the still-head temperature is around 98°C (208.5°F). This is done to recover the residual alcohol, which is propagated to future runs.

If the distillation is being done in a fractionating-still, the tails phase can be finished up in a purge mode of operation. This is done to more efficiently recover the residual alcohol in the boiler. After the tails phase has started and the head temperature has risen about 2°C (4°F), the output valve can be closed and the still left to equilibrate for a few minutes. This concentrates the remaining alcohol to the top of the column. The output valve can then be opened and the alcohol drawn off. This is called purging the still of the last residual alcohol, and will be explained in more detail in *Chapter 9 Distillation Methods*.

Feints: The tails are mixed with the heads and are called "feints". Feints are saved and recycled in future spirit-runs.

As the feints are repeatedly recycled through spirit-run after spirit-run, they become more and more richly imbued with the desirable whiskey congeners, so each batch of whiskey is incrementally improved over the previous.

When distillers run their first batch, when they have no feints yet, the whiskey flavour is reasonably good but the middle-run is comparatively small so the yield is much lower than for the following runs. But as they run subsequent batches, carrying over the feints from their previous batches, the whiskey gets better and better with each batch.

Most distillers do not recycle all the feints on-hand through subsequent spirit-runs. They include a certain measure, and each distiller's measure becomes a main part of the unique signature of that distiller's whiskey. Another important part of defining a particular distiller's unique product is when the begin- and end-cuts are made for the middle-run.

As a general rule the begin-cut of the middle-run is made when the percent alcohol of the emerging distillate is down to 80%, and the end-cut is made at 65%. However, this can vary based on preference and on the still. For example, the fractionating still described in this text tends to favour a later end-cut, sometimes as low as 59% when considerable proportions of malt or rye are used.

In most whiskey-producing countries, the begin-cut percentages are predicated by law at 80% or less. However notwithstanding the law, if a distiller wants the whiskey to have more flavour or bite, the begin-cut can be made a little earlier (ie Above 80%). And for less flavour or bite, the begin-cut can be made a little later (ie Below 80%).

The end-cut is made when the distillate loses its sweetness and desirable flavour. Novice distillers can simply end-cut the middle-run and switch to the tails phase at 65%, or a little less, until they learn to recognize the flavour characteristics of the end-cut.

There are three ways that the begin- and end-cuts are determined. The original method was by taste. Distillers would taste the distillate as it came out of the still to determine when to make the cuts. And in fact, as one learns to make whiskey they will invariably learn these taste characteristics even as they employ other methods of determining the cuts.

The second and most common method, and by far the most systematic, is to measure the percent alcohol of the emerging distillate. Commercial distilleries use this method but they reserve the final decision to taste.

The third method is by observing the still-head temperature. Unfortunately, there are so many variables that can influence the still-head temperature that this is not a reliable method. However, it does give a good indication as to when to anticipate the cuts. For example, the begin-cut takes place around 91 or 92°C (196 or 198°F), and the end-cut takes place around 94 to 95°C (201 to 203°F). As the still-head temperature approaches these levels, the distiller can start measuring percent alcohol or tasting the distillate.

However, for small operations such as we are concerned with, it's difficult to get an accurate measure of the percent alcohol of samples that are small enough to be useful in determining the cuts. Doing spirit runs of larger quantities of accumulated low wines minimizes this difficulty. The larger the run, the longer the transitions are from one cut to the next making them easier to measure. Using an alcohol refractometer is a good way to go here. Refractometers don't tend to be all that precise but their precision is good enough to give excellent results.

Also, the specially-made narrow proof-hydrometer cylinder detailed in *Chapter 4 Equipment* can enable a distiller to accurately measure the percent alcohol of a 50 to 70mL sample of distillate. This is even a little too large a sample to begin-cut a spirit run of low wines from a single 20L batch of mash. The distiller really needs to beer-strip four to six 20L batches of mash and then do a spirit run on all of them together. Or, fewer batches if a good measure of feints is included.

A novice distiller doing a single batch without a refractometer can begin-cut using a narrow-cylinder proof hydrometer by cutting to the middle-run when a 70mL sample reads 85%. This is because the end of the 70mL sample would be down around 80%. The trick is to time the taking of the sample. If the begin-cut is missed, the distiller can simply close the output valve and return the heads to the still and start over. However, after a few tries the novice distiller will learn to recognize the begin-cut by taste.

In order to facilitate this familiarization with recognizing the cuts, tables are provided later in the text with times, flow rates, phases, volumes, head temperatures, and percent alcohol measurements for actual distillation runs of batches of corn mash using the equipment and recipes detailed in the previous chapters. This puts the distiller in the correct ballpark for each cut so they can familiarize themselves with the taste changes that occur across the transitions.

Even in this modern day of advanced instrumentation, commercial whiskey distillers still rely on tasting the emerging distillate to do the final determination of the cuts.

As for the dimension of whiskey flavour contributed by the proportion of feints added to the spirit-run, the more feints the more body and richness the whiskey flavour will have. In effect, the feints don't change the whiskey's flavour, but rather contribute more of it.

After numerous spirit-runs, more and more feints will accumulate. At some point, the distiller can do a special spirit-run on the accumulated feints alone. Many distillers contend that the whiskey produced by this special run is the smoothest, richest, most flavourful whiskey of all, and it is often escalated to the status of the distiller's "Special Reserve" or "The Queen's own cask".

And finally, the feature that is reputed to impart the most unique signature on the whiskey flavour is the spirit still itself. There's a certain mystique surrounding this dimension, because no one appears to have a complete explanation why there's such a profound difference between whiskey distilled in one still and whiskey distilled in another apparently identical still. It's likely to be a combination of the height of the column, the width of the column, the distribution of the heat, and so on. When single-malt whiskey distilleries fabricate new stills they replicate their old stills right down to duplicating every dent or kink or irregularity in thickness of the copper wall, to minimize any difference a new still may have over the old stills.

OPERATING PROCEDURES FOR DISTILLATION

This section describes the various procedures required to fill and drain the still, operate the ancillary equipment, and perform a beer stripping run.

<u>Transferring the Mash to the Still</u>: After the mash has been strained it can be transferred to the still. However, it's useful to cover the strained mash and allow it to settle for 12 or 24 hours. This will allow the suspended yeast and very fine mash solids to settle out, leaving a clear yellow liquid, with the suspended solids packed down to a sediment about 8 cm (3") deep. The clear liquid can be siphoned off the sediment into another container, or directly into the still.

This is important because if there's too much sediment suspended in the mash there's the risk that it will burn against the immersion element and spoil the flavour of the whiskey. This is of particular concern when using a 1500W element. Fortunately, grain mash settles out very well in a matter of only a few hours.

If the mash is very cloudy with a lot of suspended solids, it may be necessary to put a 750W element in the boiler for the particular beer-stripping run to prevent burning against the immersion element.

To transfer the mash to the still place the mash container about half a meter to a meter (1½' to 3') above the top of the boiler. Connect the filler-hose to the bottom ball valve on the still. Open the bottom ball valve (make sure the top one is closed), and place the siphon starter in the mash. Pump the siphon starter until the siphon starts. Allow the mash to run into the still. When it's finished, remove the siphon hose from the siphon starter and blow into it to push the last contents of the hose into the boiler, and close the ball valve while still blowing. The filler hose can then be removed from the ball valve.

Transferring Low Wines to the Still: Low wines are transferred to the still in exactly the same manner as described above for the mash.

If an adjunct of feints is to be included in a spirit run, it should be mixed with the low wines before siphoning into the still.

Low wines are typically about 40 to 50% ethanol. This concentration of ethanol will dissolve acrylic. Unfortunately, a lot of home winemaking equipment, such as siphon starters, are made of acrylic and cannot be used in contact with low wines.

In the event that you can't find a siphon starter made of alcohol-resistant material, the low wines can be transferred to the still by placing the filler-hose in the low wines with the siphon-starter removed. Next, open the bottom ball valve (ensure the top one is closed), and suck on the end of the filler-hose with the garden-hose fitting. When the filler-hose is nearly full of low wines, pinch the tube, and quickly screw the fitting to the upper ball valve. After the fitting is secure, release the pinch on the tube and the low wines will flow into the still.
This will likely require more than one try, and may result in a small spill of low wines.

Before long, you should be able to locate an alcohol-resistant siphon starter.

Measuring Alcohol Content: Measuring alcohol content is done by using an instrument called a "proof hydrometer". A proof hydrometer is essentially measuring the Specific Gravity (SG) of the liquid but presents the reading on two scales: alcohol percentage; and, alcohol proof. They're calibrated based on the assumption that the liquid being measured is a mixture of ethanol and water and nothing else. And, for distilled spirits this is a very safe assumption. It's important to note that a proof hydrometer cannot be used to measure the alcohol content of mash, wine, beer, or any undistilled form of beverage alcohol. Such beverages contain residual sugars and acids and many other compounds that radically alter the SG, and hence a proof-hydrometer measurement.

In this text the term "proof" as a unit of alcohol content has been avoided in favour of "percent alcohol". There are at least three different proof scales, and each one requires mental arithmetic in order to be meaningful. So, for simplicity all references to alcohol content will be expressed as percent alcohol by volume (ie. % abv).

To use a proof hydrometer, place the hydrometer in the empty cylinder and fill the cylinder with enough spirit to float the hydrometer, then read the alcohol content off the percent alcohol scale.

Alcohol volume is very sensitive to thermal expansion and contraction. Proof hydrometers are usually calibrated at 20°C (68°F) and a variation of only a few degrees from this temperature will skew the measurement noticeably. So, to obtain an accurate measurement, the temperature of the sample must be either adjusted to 20°C (68°F) or the reading corrected using the *Proof-Hydrometer Temperature Correction Table* at *Appendix B*.

An alcohol refractometer is very convenient for measuring the alcohol content of the emerging distillate because it not only requires a very small sample (ie. 3 drops) but the sample cools to ambient temperature almost immediately. This is particularly useful for small-scale distillation where the cuts transition very quickly with relatively low volumes of distillate.

Beer Stripping: The first step is to do a crude primary distillation on the corn mash. This can be done using a beer stripper as described in *Chapter 4 Equipment*, or by simply using the spirit still with the needle valve set to a very high flow rate to effect a primary distillation.

The purpose of the beer stripping is largely to facilitate the operational efficiency of the process. It enables a large volume of mash to be reduced to a more manageable volume of higher percent abv to be processed in the spirit still. A distiller will typically save the low wines from several beer-stripping runs, then do one big spirit-run on the accumulated low wines, this way contending with only one set of cuts between phases of a single larger run.

As mentioned above, beer stripping can either be done using a beer stripper or by using the spirit still. Transfer the strained corn mash to the boiler, close both ball valves, start running cold water through the heat exchanger, and turn on the electric current. Place a suitably sized receiver under the output and open the needle valve approximately half way.

You will be collecting between 3 and 3½L of low wines for every 20L of 8% abv mash placed in the still. With a 3000W element, 60L of mash will come to boil in less than two hours. With a 750W element, 20L of mash will come to boil in less than 3½ hours, and 40L will come to boil in about 5½ hours. After it comes to boil and the low wines have begun to drip from the needle valve, adjust the needle valve so the distillate is flowing at noticeably less than the maximum rate. This minimizes the amount of alcohol left in the still at the end of the run by affording a certain level of reflux and, thereby, better separation.

The temperature of the vapour coming over from the boiler at the start will be about 80°C (176°F) and will rise to 98°C (208.4°F) or so as the ethanol in the boiler is depleted. Although there will be a little ethanol remaining in the boiler at 98°C (208.4°F), the amount will be too small to warrant the cost of electricity or the time to drive over. 60L will take a total of about 12 hours with a 3000W element, 20L will take a total of about 11 or 12 hours with a 750W element, and 40L will take about 20 hours with a 750W element. These may seem like long times but beer stripping runs largely unattended.

Distillers who are familiar with using fractionating stills to do beer stripping of straight sugar-and-water mashes to make neutral alcohol, will likely have learned that by running the distillation at lower flow rates, they receive low wines with higher concentrations of alcohol. That is to say, that with a fractionating still the same amount of alcohol is received in the same time period regardless of the flow rate. It's simply a matter of: the lower the flow rate the higher the concentration of alcohol; and the higher the flow rate the lower the concentration. It's the same amount of alcohol in different overall volumes. This inverse proportion, however, does not hold for flow rates that are so low that the alcohol concentration is over 95%. The reason for this is that as the alcohol concentration approaches the theoretical maximum of 96.5% (ie. the alcohol-water azeotrope), the concentration can't increase no matter how high the reflux ratio is. So, slowing the flow rate beyond that point will not increase the concentration, but will only slow the rate of alcohol received.

However, distillers who are beer stripping for the purpose of making whiskey must resist any temptation to slow the flow rate down to achieve low wines with a higher alcohol concentration, because this results in the fractionating still stripping out too much of the congeners that are important to the flavour profile of the whiskey.

Low wines for whiskey should be between 40 and 50% alcohol. If near the end of a beer-stripping run the low wines are much above this range, turn the flow rate up a little and continue the run until the total alcohol concentration of the run is down within that range.

CHAPTER 9

DISTILLATION METHODS

In this chapter, methods of doing the spirit-run that produce the finished whiskey are described. Because of the exacting nature of the descriptions, the procedures will stay closely focused on the distillation of 20L batches of the fermented corn mash produced in the previous chapters, and on using the fractionating still described in *Chapter 4 Equipment*.

After all the batches of mash that are going into this run have been beer-stripped, load the low wines into the spirit still. There must be at least 5L of liquid in the still to ensure the heating element is immersed at all times. If there are less that 8L of low wines, simply top the volume of low wines up to 8L or so with water. 8L ensures there will still be 5L in the still at the end of the spirit-run. This will make no difference to the flavour or quality of the finished whiskey.

An adjunct of feints should be mixed with the low wines before it's loaded in the still. 4L makes a good proportion for the low wines from up to four 20L batches of corn mash. However, if this is the first time you have ever done a spirit-run you won't have any feints to add. This is alright, you can go ahead and do the distillation without feints. The flavour of the whiskey will be good, but the middle-run will be smaller so the yield will be much lower than when you have feints.

The output from the spirit-run should be carefully recorded in a table such as the one in Table 1 (overleaf). A blank copy of this table is provided as *Appendix C* and can be photocopied for this purpose.

TIME	Rate of flow (ml/min)	PHASE	Amount Collected (ml)	Amount Collected (Corrected to 100% alc)	Amount Left (ml of 100% alc/vol)	Stillhead Temp °C	% Alcohol of Emerging Distillate	% Alcohol of Aggregate
07:00	0	E	0	0	2,035	78.5		

Table 1

The percent alcohol of the *Amount-Collected* values recorded in Table 1 will vary from the beginning to the end of the run. However, they will stay approximately consistent from one run to the next. For example, the percent alcohol of the heads will be roughly the same for two different runs if they are both distilled using the same regimen.

Once the still is loaded, calculate how much alcohol at 100% is in the still so Table 1 can be initialized. The following are two examples of how the volume of 100% alcohol of the Low Wines (LW) is calculated: one with no feints; and, one with 3.2L of feints:

Without feints:
    Vol LW x % alc of LW = Vol @ 100% alc in the still

    21900mL x 0.40 = **8,765mL** @ 100% alc

With feints:
 (Vol LW x % alc of LW) + (Vol feints x % alc of feints) = Vol of 100% alc in still

(20,500mL x 0.43) + (6500mL x 0.66) = **13,100**mL of 100% alc

Tables 2 and 3 have been initialized with these values as examples. Both examples are of spirit-runs performed on the accumulated low wines from five 20L batches of mash.

Actual data from a spirit-run of 21900mL of low wines (1500W)
(40% alcohol, no adjunct of feints)

21900mL x 0.40 = **8765**mL alcohol @ 100%

TIME	Rate of flow (ml/min)	PHASE	Amount Collected (ml)	Amount Collected (Corrected to 100% alc)	Amount Left (ml of 100% alc/vol)	Stillhead Temp °C	% Alcohol of Emerging Distillate	% Alcohol of Aggregate
10:20	0	E	0	0	**8,765**	78.5		
11:55	45	H	3,500	2,940	5,825	89.2	80	84
14:00	35	MR	4,595	3,400	2,425	94.5	65	74
15:45	various	T&P	3,000	1,380	1,045	97.4		46

Table 2

Actual data from a spirit-run of 20,500mL of low wines (1500W)
(43% alcohol with a 6,500mL adjunct of feints @ 66% alcohol)

(20,500mL x 0.43) + (6,500 x 0.66) = **13,100**mL alcohol @ 100%

TIME	Rate of flow (ml/min)	PHASE	Amount Collected (ml)	Amount Collected (Corrected to 100% alc)	Amount Left (ml of 100% alc/vol)	Stillhead Temp °C	% Alcohol of Emerging Distillate	% Alcohol of Aggregate
10:40	0	E	0	0	**13,100**	78.5		
13:00	45	H	5,110	4,395	3,640	89	80	86
16:40	35	MR	7,360	5,080	2,415	95	65	69
19:10	various	T&P	4,040	2,060	525	98		51

Table 3

In the *Phase* columns of Tables 2 and 3 there are four phases indicated: E for Equilibration; H for Heads; MR for Middle-Run; and T&P for Tails and Purge.

In order to use the tables at Tables 2 and 3 as accurate guides for the cuts for your spirit runs, it is necessary to map the quantities on these tables to the one you are using for your quantities.

For instance, Table 3 shows a total volume of 100% alcohol of 13,100mL. Say the volume of 100% alcohol in a particular run of yours was 13,625mL. A mapping factor can be calculated by dividing your volume by Table 3's volume.
That is, $13,625 \div 13,100 = 1.04$.

The *Amount Collected* (100% alc) column in Table 3 shows the total volumes for each phase. Multiply these volumes by the mapping factor, 1.04, and enter the results in the corresponding column of a copy of the table at *Appendix C*.

This copy can be used as a reference to enable you to very closely emulate the results of the actual spirit run documented by Table 3.

Having such a table as a guideline can be very reassuring to a novice distiller just becoming familiar with judging the cuts.

Using Tables 2 or 3, depending on whether your run has an adjunct of feints or not, follow the example given above for Table 3 and enter volumes for each phase into a copy of the table at *Appendix C*. You are now ready to begin your spirit run. Use another copy of the table at *Appendix C* to record the actual results of your spirit run.

FRACTIONATING-STILL METHOD

The fractionating-still method is a means of using a high-separation fractionating still to make flavour-positive spirits such as whiskey or schnapps. This method employs the ability to vary the level of separation in a fractionating still by increasing or decreasing the reflux ratio, which is done by varying the flow rate.

In the case of a flavour-positive spirit the reflux ratio must be reduced considerably from the level used to produce pure alcohol (eg. 90% reflux). The reflux ratio shouldn't be more than 50 or 60%, and can be as low as almost 0%. The real question is whether you can manage the cuts between the phases at such high flow rates. The high flow rates are much less of a problem when running the still to full capacity with low wines and producing larger volumes of whiskey. These larger runs have much longer transitions from one phase to the next so the cuts are much easier to judge.

With the still filled and both ball valves closed, start running cold water through the heat exchangers, ensure the needle valve is closed, place a 250mL graduated cylinder under the output, turn on the electric current, and wait for it to boil. With a 1500W element, 20L of low wines will take about an hour and 45 minutes to come to boil.

When it comes to boil the still-head thermometer will read about 78°C (172.5°F). Since there is no need to equilibrate the column when making whiskey, the needle valve can be opened right away. Adjust the needle valve until the flow rate is about 40 or 50% of maximum. A 1500W element typically gives a maximum flow rate of about 100mL per minute, and a 750W element gives a maximum flow rate of about 50mL per minute. This is not a critical adjustment but it's important that the flow rate not be too low for a fractionating still or it will just strip the pure alcohol out of the substrate and leave all the whiskey flavours behind with the rest of the congeners.

If you're following the tables at Table 2 or 3 and if you're using a 1500W element, just adjust it to 45mL/minute. It's best to run the heads a little faster and then slow it down for the middle-run. This is the heads phase and the distillate from this phase should be collected in a container labeled "heads".

At this decreased level of separation, there will be no discreet foreshots phase per se, so the emerging distillate at this point will be the heads phase, which will include the foreshots.

It's best not to taste the emerging spirit at the beginning of the heads phase since the foreshots are present in them. The solvent-like smell will easily warn you off doing this at this point. Shortly after the beginning of the heads phase the solvent-like smell will dissipate and you can begin tasting the emerging spirit periodically so as to become familiar with the begin-cut. To taste the emerging spirit, collect a few drops on a spoon.

For 20L of low wines with no adjunct of feints, you can expect about 3,500mL of heads before the begin-cut to the middle-run. Using your table, mapped from Table 2 or 3, you can estimate roughly how much heads to expect before cutting to the middle-run. It helps to know approximately what volume to expect so you'll have some idea of when to begin measuring the percent alcohol of the evolving distillate to determine the begin-cut. The still-head temperature will stay around 78.5 to 79°C (173 to 174°F) for the first few minutes, then it will begin to rise. The begin-cut will occur at about 89 or 90°C (192 or 194°F), just before the temperature stabilizes at about 91°C (196°F). So, keep in mind that switching receivers to the middle-run is done before the temperature stabilizes.

As soon as you observe the temperature to rise from about 79°C (174°F), begin taking measurements of the percent alcohol emerging from the still. This is where an alcohol refractometer comes in handy. It can measure a sample of about 3 drops, whereas a narrow-cylinder proof-hydrometer requires from 50 to 70mL.

The Liebig condenser will keep the temperature of the distillate running from the still fairly constant for the duration of the run, so you should measure it early in the run and find the temperature correction on the *Proof-Hydrometer Temperature Correction Table* at *Appendix B*, so you'll be able to make the correction at a glance when you're getting close to the cuts.

As the still-head temperature increases, the percent alcohol of the emerging spirit decreases. The begin-cut must be made when the percent alcohol has decreased to 80%. If you miss this cut, close the needle valve and pour all the distillate back into the still through the top of the heat exchanger, and wait about a minute and then start over. If the still chokes after pouring the distillate back in, just unplug it for a minute and then plug it back in after it settles back down.

Remember, that for a small batch of low wines from a single 20L batch of mash if you're using a narrow-cylinder proof-hydrometer, when the 50 to 70mL sample reads 85%, the emerging distillate will be down to about 80%. Also, be sure to use the temperature-correction table at *Appendix B* to correct the proof-hydrometer reading.

On a larger run, such as the examples at Tables 2 and 3, when the emerging distillate is down to 80%, empty the contents of the receiver into the middle-run container, and begin collecting the middle-run. On a smaller run when the emerging distillate is down to 85%, as explained above, empty the contents into the heads container, and begin collecting the middle-run.

Immediately after switching to the middle-run, adjust the flow rate down to 35mL/minute.

Once you have switched to the middle-run receiver, measure the total volume of the heads and their aggregate percent alcohol, and record these in the spirit-run record. Be sure to transfer the heads to a container clearly labeled "Corn Feints" and store them for future spirit-runs.

At this point the process is in the middle-run phase. Again, referring to your table, determine roughly how much middle-run to expect before switching to the tails phase.

With most whiskey stills the middle-run ends when the percent alcohol of the emerging distillate has decreased to about 65%. However, with a fractionating still this end-cut can often be lower. Ultimately, this is decided by taste. Throughout the middle-run the emerging distillate will taste sweet, smooth, and pleasant. But, as the middle-run comes to the end, the flavour becomes watery and the sweetness gives way to a harsh, bitter, and unpleasant taste. Novice distillers, until they learn to recognize this flavour change, can simply switch to the tails phase when the emerging distillate drops to 65%. At this point, the still-head temperature will be about 94 or 95°C (201 or 203°F). After switching to the tails phase, the distillate should be collected in a container labeled "tails".

However, it's important for novice distillers to continue tasting the emerging distillate after this early switch to tails in order to become familiar with the above-mentioned flavour changes at the end-cut.

After the middle-run is completed, make sure that the entire middle-run is placed in a single container and thoroughly mixed. This, when diluted, is the finished corn whiskey.

Measure the total volume of the middle-run and its aggregate percent alcohol, and record these in the spirit-run record.

The remaining distillate is the tails and should be collected until the still-head temperature is about 98°C (208.5°F). With a fractionating still, the remainder of the alcohol in the still can be very efficiently purged by closing the needle valve and allowing the still to equilibrate. After a few minutes the still-head temperature will drop to about 78.5°C (173°F). At this point, the needle valve can be opened to about 3 to 5 drops per second (ie. 30 to 50 drops per 10 seconds). When the temperature rises to about 83 or 84°C (181 or 183°F), the needle valve can be closed and the still left for a few minutes to equilibrate again, then the needle valve opened to 3 to 5 drops per second. This can be repeated a number of times until the still takes too long to equilibrate back down to 78.5°C (173°F) to be practical to continue. This marks the end of the tails-and-purge phase, and of the entire run. This purging can begin when the still-head temperature is around 97°C (206.5°F).

Measure the total volume of the tails and their aggregate percent alcohol, and record these in the spirit-run record. Be sure to transfer the tails to the container labeled "Corn Feints" where they are mixed with the heads. The heads and the tails combined are the feints that are stored for future spirit-runs.

Do not empty the residue out of the boiler until you are sure you are satisfied with the whiskey. If you inadvertently spoil the middle-run by misjudging the begin- or end-cuts, you can simply return the heads, middle-run (diluted or not), and tails to the residue in the boiler and redo the entire spirit-run.

The spirit-run can be rerun in this manner several times if required, which is often necessary for a novice distiller becoming familiar with the cuts. This rerun can even be done when a significant portion of the middle-run has been consumed during evaluation. The middle-run cut will just be smaller.

In the tables at Tables 2 and 3, which are data from actual spirit-runs, you will observe that each run records a loss of alcohol around 10-14%. This loss is almost entirely due to alcohol left in the boiler after the still is switched off.

When the spirit-run is complete the packing in the column will be flooded with tails. These should be thoroughly washed from the column by pouring generous quantities of boiling water down from the top.

Next, the boiler should be drained and flushed. This can be done by attaching the drain-hose to the bottom ball valve and leading the tube to a floor drain then opening the valve. After the boiler has drained it can be flushed by attaching one end of the flushing-hose to the upper ball valve and the other to a tap with a garden-hose thread. Open the upper ball valve and turn on the tap for a few seconds, let it drain, turn on the tap again, let it drain, and so on until it's flushed.

Flow Rate: The flow rate for a whiskey run using a fractionating still is typically around 40 or 50% of the maximum flow rate for the still. However, it's best to run the still a little faster during the heads phase in order to ensure the begin-cut happens before too much alcohol has passed through. As mentioned earlier, it's important not to run a fractionating still too slow during the heads phase when making whiskey or the begin-cut will never occur. This is because the percent alcohol of the emerging distillate won't drop to 80% until almost all the alcohol has passed through (ie. it'll just strip the alcohol out of the low wines). You can tell if the flow rate is too low if the temperature fails to rise above about 78.5 or 79°C (173 or 174°F).

A typical example of too low a flow rate (ie. too high a level of separation) would be if 40 or 50% of the total alcohol had run through and the percent alcohol of the evolving distillate were still above 80%, leaving the run stuck in the heads phase. If this occurs, the still should be shut down, all the distillate returned to the boiler, and the run started over at a higher flow rate. For example, if the flow rate were 45mL per minute during the heads phase, then it could be raised to 55mL per minute.

After the begin-cut is made, the flow rate can be slowed down to ensure a smooth, clean middle-run. For example, for a 1500W element you can take the heads off at 45mL per minute and slow it down to 35mL per minute for the middle-run and tails.

The optimum flow rates remain very consistent from run to run for a given still, so once you've worked out the best flow rates for your set-up, they will remain the same for subsequent runs.

As mentioned above, with small runs like a single 20L batch of mash, the cuts will come by fast and you will have to pay close attention to avoid misjudging them. However, larger runs will have longer transitions and will be much easier to judge at the higher flow rates. Naturally, higher flow rates and larger runs, scale nicely to larger operations.

Diluting: The final stage in making corn whiskey is to dilute the middle-run to between 40 and 50% alc/vol. It's a good idea to use distilled or de-ionized water as sold at supermarkets and pharmacies to dilute corn whiskey. However, many people simply use soft or filtered tap water.

Hard water should be avoided because, not only can it impart off flavours, but it can cast a white precipitate that often results in a turbid or cloudy appearance, or a chalky sediment at the bottom of the bottle. This precipitate is perfectly harmless, but is aesthetically unpleasing.

An example of diluting the middle-run to produce an excellent corn whiskey is to mix 2385mL of 70% middle-run with 1325mL of distilled water to produce 3710mL of 45% alc/vol corn whiskey.

A formula to use for calculating the amount of water needed to dilute the middle-run (MR) to the desired percent alcohol is as follows:

(Vol of MR x % alc of MR) ÷ (Desired % alc - Vol of MR) = Vol of water required

Eg. (2385ml x 70%) ÷ (45% - 2385ml) = 1325ml

Blending: Whiskey produced in a high-separation fractionating still tends to have a very rich and intense flavour profile. This is because high-separation stills concentrate more of the desirable congeners into the middle-run while keeping the undesirable ones out, as opposed to lower-separation stills which lose more of the desirable congeners to the heads and the tails in the course of keeping the undesirable ones out. In the end, whiskey made in a high-separation still is clean and rich.

Most people like, or come to like, this intense flavour. However, the intensity can be reduced if desired.

There are several ways to reduce the intensity of the flavour. One is to blend the whiskey with grain-neutral. Grain-neutral is about 95% abv and is, for all practical purposes, pure alcohol that is very nearly devoid of all congeners. See *Chapter 11 Pure-Ethanol Distillation* on how to make grain-neutral.

The grain-neutral should be diluted with pure water to the same alcohol content as the whiskey. A small sample, say 30mL (1 oz), of the whiskey can be blended 50:50 with diluted grain-neutral and tasted. If the flavour has become too insipid or is still too intense, the ratio can be adjusted slightly and tasted again. This is repeated until the desired blend is achieved.

However, purists can quite rightly argue that once blended with grain-neutral, pure corn whiskey is no longer pure. So, in order to reduce flavour intensity without violating the purity of the whiskey, the distillation process must be adjusted.

A narrower cut can be taken. That is to say, let the heads run a little later and end the middle-run a little earlier. This way less congeners go into the middle-run and therefore the flavour is less intense.

Storage: Distilled spirits should be stored in glass, not plastic. Corn whiskey, by tradition, does not require aging in oak or charred oak barrels. Pure corn whiskey can be consumed right away. However, many distillers including the author contend that corn whiskey does improve for about five weeks after it's made. The same, by the way, is also true for other non-aged spirits such as gin and vodka, and most producers of these spirits ensure their product is not shipped for about three months after bottling.

However, if the spirit were not distilled properly, for example if too much tails were allowed to pervade into the middle-run, this brief aging period would only amplify the off flavours.

Until recently no-one appeared to have an explanation for how this aging worked, and many people believed it was just folklore. However, scientists have discovered that when a mixture of compounds is first made, the molecules of the individual compounds form clusters and don't completely diffuse throughout the mixture, but over time the clusters slowly break apart and eventually become evenly dispersed throughout the mixture. This process of diffusing the molecules of all the compounds results in a smoothing and maturing of the flavour.

Experimentation has revealed that this process of diffusing the clusters of molecules can be greatly accelerated by subjecting such mixtures to a certain optimum frequency of vibration that promotes the diffusion of their molecules.

It's interesting to note that back in the 1700s it was observed and recorded that sloshing whiskey around in barrels by transporting it by mule for hundreds of miles had a distinctly lubricous effect on the flavour of the whiskey. Perhaps the sloshing resulted in a diffusion of the clusters of molecules.

Vibrating devices specifically designed for aging alcoholic beverages have even been developed and are for sale, but it's certainly much too early to conclude that this principle is even valid let alone to recommend devices that exploit it.

POT-STILL METHOD

Some distillers contend that this pot-still method yields a more delicate and desirable whiskey flavour than the fractionating-still method. Some also say the flavour tends to be less intense. In any case, the flavour is noticeably different between the two methods.

The pot-still method is a means of making a fractionating still emulate a pot still. In its normal mode of operation a fractionating still has vapour rising up the column that condenses at the top and flows back down through the packing where it encounters the rising vapour causing reflux. The flow rate is controlled by a valve that redirects a proportion of the condensate to the output tube.

In a pot still there is no systematic process of reflux other than what condenses naturally and falls back down against the rising vapour. All the vapour that reaches the top of the column, or the vapour chamber, is directed to a condenser and then outside the still. The flow rate is controlled by varying the amount of heat to the boiler.

In this pot-still method, the fractionating still is fitted with a potentiometer that serves as a heat control. As discussed in *Chapter 4 Equipment*, the most common form of potentiometer for this purpose is a lighting dimmer switch. Please make sure that if you're using a dimmer switch that it's rated for the power output of the heating element in the boiler. For example, the standard dimmer switches sold in hardware stores are typically rated for 600W. If your still has a 750W element, then a 600W dimmer switch is not suitable and will burn out. In this case, you would have to use a 1000W dimmer switch generally found at specialty lighting or electrical stores.

With a fractionating still fitted with a heat control, the still is operated with the output valve wide open, and the heat control is used to vary the flow rate to the desired level. In this manner (ie. with the output valve wide open) virtually all of the condensed vapour is directed outside the still, so no liquid is available to flow back down the column to reflux against the rising vapour. This way the vapour is rising up the column, being condensed, and exiting the still, with very little reflux. This is functionally how a pot still operates.

This method of operation can also be applied to other still designs such as the popular reflux stills that many people have, or actual whiskey stills. Or even, real pot stills. Many of these other stills are burner-top models, and the heat to the boiler is controlled by adjusting the burner setting.

If you are using a burner to heat the still, it can be quite beneficial to fit the burner with a potentiometer. The idea being, to set the burner control to maximum and then use the potentiometer to control the power to the burner. This avoids the constant turning on and off that most burners do when turned to an intermediate setting. Using a potentiometer in this manner delivers a smooth, consistent heat to the still.

To operate using the pot-still method, set the still up exactly as is done for the fractionating-still method above. Initially, it's most convenient to leave the output valve closed until the still comes to a full boil. This relieves the operator of having to be there at the moment it begins to boil. However, if a fractionating still comes to boil and is left for any period of time with the output valve closed it will equilibrate. Equilibration is deleterious to whiskey distillation because it strips out too much of the congeners. If this happens, turn the still off for a couple of minutes to break the equilibration cycle before opening the output valve. Then open the valve up all the way and turn the still back on.

It's important to note that changes in the heat-control setting will take a few minutes to effect changes in flow rate, so adjustments in flow rate should be done gradually and patiently.

Once the still is boiling and the desired flow rate has been established with the heat control, the rest of the distillation process is identical to that of the fractionating-still method.

SUMMARY OF PROCEDURES

The following is a consolidated summary of the procedures used to make pure corn whiskey that were detailed in *Chapter 6 Mashing*, *Chapter 7 Fermentation*, and *Chapter 9 Distillation Methods*.

MASHING

1. Prepare 23L of pH 5.8 mash water in a large pot on a stove.
2. Turn the stove on high.
3. Monitor the temperature until it's 74°C (165°F).
4. Turn off the heat, and stir in 4Kg (8.8 lbs) of flaked maize.
5. Stir the mash until the starches disperse, and the temperature drops to 66.5°C (152°F).
6. Stir in ¾Kg (1.65 lbs) of crushed barley malt.
7. Cover and leave for 90 minutes or longer.

FERMENTATION

8. Measure the OG of the mash.
9. Ensure OG is below 1.070 (ie. ideally between 1.060 and 1.070). Adjust with water if necessary.
10. Ensure mash temperature is below 38°C (100°F). Chill if necessary.
11. Transfer the mash to a 30+L fermenter.
12. Aerate the mash.
13. Ensure ambient temperature is between 21°C and 33°C (70°F and 90°F).
14. Pitch 60gm(1/3 cup) active dried distillers' yeast plus 1 tsp distillery glucoamylase
    Or
    1 package of whiskey yeast / enzyme combination
15. Allow to ferment to completion (typically, 72 to 84 hours).
16. Strain the mash.
17. Measure the TG of the mash.
18. Measure the volume of the mash.
19. Calculate the percent abv of the mash.

BEER-STRIPPING DISTILLATION

20. Transfer the fermented and strained corn mash to the still.
21. Close both ball valves.
22. Start running cold water through the condenser.
23. Turn on the electric current.
24. Place a suitably sized receiver under the output of the beer stripper.
25. Collect the low wines until the still-head temperature reaches about 98°C (208.4°F).

SPIRIT-RUN

26. Add an adjunct of feints to the low wines from the beer-stripping run.
27. Transfer the low wines to the spirit still.
28. Ensure spirit still contains at least 8L. Top up with water if necessary.
29. Close both ball valves.
30. Calculate the volume of 100% abv in the still and enter it into a spirit-run table copied from *Appendix C*.
31. Map the Table 2 or 3 volumes to your volumes and enter them in your spirit-run table.
32. Start running cold water through the heat exchanger.
33. Ensure the needle valve is closed.
34. Place a 250mL graduated cylinder under the output.
35. Turn on the electric current.
36. Wait for it to boil. With a 1500W element, 20L of low wines will take about 1¾ hours.
37. After it comes to boil leave the needle valve closed for a minute or so to let the still come to a complete boil.
38. Foreshots & Heads: Open the needle valve and adjust the flow rate to 45mL per minute.
39. Using the mapped volumes from your table, estimate roughly how much heads to expect.
40. Determine the end of the heads phase by measuring the percent alcohol of the emerging distillate. When it drops to 80% switch to the middle-run.
41. Middle-run: Transfer all the heads to a container labeled "Corn Feints" and begin collecting the middle-run. Reduce the flow rate to 35mL per minute

42. Using the mapped volumes from your table, estimate roughly how much middle-run to expect.
43. Towards the end of the middle-run, measure the percent alcohol of the emerging distillate. When it drops to 65% switch to the tails.
44. Tails: Collect the tails until the still-head temperature is about 98°C (208.5°F). Purge the remaining alcohol if using a fractionating still.
45. Switch off the still.
46. Transfer all the tails to the container labeled "Corn Feints".
47. Place the entire middle-run in a single container and mix thoroughly.
48. Flush the column with boiling water.
49. Drain and flush the boiler.
50. Dilute the middle-run to between 40 and 50% abv with distilled or deionized water.
51. The diluted middle-run is the finished corn whiskey, and can be consumed right away. However, the flavour will benefit by aging for up to five weeks in glass.

CHAPTER 11

PURE-ETHANOL DISTILLATION

After distilling for a while you will invariably accrue an appreciable quantity of excess heads and tails, experimental distillations that you've abandoned, and other forms of left-over ethanol that you have no intention of drinking, all collected in containers labeled "redistill".

The best thing to do with redistill, as the name implies, is to redistil it and rectify it into pure ethanol to be made into vodka, gin, or essence-based spirits.

To distil pure ethanol, you need a high-separation fractionating still such as the one detailed in *Chapter 4 Equipment*. Pot stills are not suitable for making pure ethanol because they simply don't afford sufficient separation to isolate the pure ethanol.

It's best to distil pure ethanol in fairly large batches since this is operationally more convenient and tends to produce a purer product. A pure-ethanol distillation has a very long middle-run phase and runs unattended very well.

It's very easy to determine the precise amount of ethanol in the still because the volume of the redistil can be easily measured and the percent ethanol can be accurately measured using a proof hydrometer. And, since the flow rate is maintained at a fairly constant rate, it's quite easy to calculate how long a distillation run will take, thereby enabling the operator to time the start of a distillation run so that the middle-run will end at a suitable time of day for switching to the tails.

It's not unusual to load a 1500W still with 35L (37 US Quarts) of 70% abv redistil and set it to run for about 35 hours straight. Once the foreshots and heads have been dealt with and the long middle-run phase is running, a 19L (5 US Gallon) carboy can be placed under the output, and the still can be left unattended for up to 12 hours at a time since the operator knows roughly when the middle-run will end.

PROCEDURE

Before doing a pure-ethanol run, the entire still: column; packing; and, boiler, must be thoroughly cleaned and rinsed out. Rinse the still out with hot water, then make up a solution of 45mL (3 Tbsp) of citric acid in 4L (1 US Gallon) of hot water. Rinse each part with the citric acid solution and be sure to pass the solution through all tubes and surfaces that come into contact with vapour or distillate. Finally, rinse the citric acid away with hot water.

Next, measure the volume and the percent ethanol of the redistil to be loaded into the still. Remember to use the *Proof-Hydrometer Correction Table* at *Appendix B* to adjust the percent-ethanol reading of the proof hydrometer for the temperature of the redistill. The amount of ethanol will actually have to be calculated at 95% since the maximum ethanol concentration that can be produced by straight distillation is 96.5% (ie. the ethanol/water azeotrope). 95% gives a close-enough approximation of the percent ethanol evolving from the still during a pure-ethanol run.

Load the redistil into the still keeping in mind that, like low wines, it will dissolve acrylic. Remember that some siphon starters are made of acrylic and cannot be used to siphon redistill.

There must be at least 5L of liquid in the still to ensure the heating element is immersed at all times. If there are less than 8L in the still, simply top the volume up to 8L or so with water, this will ensure there's at least 5L left in the boiler when the distillation is complete. Also, do not fill the still more than 80% full of redistill. Ethanol expands considerably more when heated than water does, so to be on the safe side, don't fill a 45L boiler with more than 37L of low-wines or redistill. If it's overfilled, it'll expand and spew out the top of the column when it comes to boil.

The output from a pure-ethanol run should be carefully recorded in a Spirit-Run Record. A blank copy is provided as *Appendix C* and can be photocopied for this purpose.

Once the still is loaded, calculate how much ethanol at 95% is in the still so the Spirit-Run Record can be initialized.

The following is an example of how the volume of 95% ethanol is calculated and contains real-life data from an actual pure-ethanol run:

(Vol of Redistil x %alc) / 0.95 = Total Vol of ethanol at 95%

(36,500mL x 0.70) / 0.95 = **26,895**mL of 95% alc

The Spirit-Run Record at Table 4 (page 125) has been initialized with this value as an example. The example is for 36.5L of redistil at 70% ethanol in a 45L fractionating still with a 1500W element.

The Estimated Run Time from when the distillate begins to flow to the end of the run is calculated as follows:

Total 95% ethanol / Flowrate (ml/min) / 60 min/hour = Estimated Run Time

26,895mL / 12mL per minute / 60 minutes per hour = 37.35 hours

Note: The Estimated Run Time does not include the time the still took to come to boil and to equilibrate, which in this run took 3 hours 20 minutes.

Once the still has been loaded, the quantity of 95% ethanol has been calculated and entered in the Spirit-Run Record, and The Estimated Run Time has been determined, decide roughly when you want the middle-run to end. Based on The Estimated Run Time, determine when to power up the still such that the middle-run ends approximately when you want it to. This must be a time when you can attend to switching to the tails phase. Having done that, ensure the needle valve is completely closed, power up the still at the chosen time, and make sure the cooling water is running before boil-up occurs.

When the still comes to boil, leave the needle valve closed for the first hour. This is the equilibration phase and is when the refluxing column sets up its dynamic equilibrium whereby the different compounds become stacked in the column with the most volatile at the top. At this point the most volatile compounds are the foreshots and will need to be bled off before the ethanol can be drawn off.

After the still has been equilibrating for an hour or so, open the needle valve and adjust the flow rate to about 8 or 10mL per minute. This is the foreshots phase and the distillate flowing from the still will have a very strong solvent-like smell. The foreshots are poisonous so the flowing distillate should not be tasted at this point. The sickening smell of the foreshots would dissuade anyone from tasting them anyway.

The foreshots should be discarded or collected in a separate container marked "poisonous".

After awhile the smell of the foreshots will diminish considerably, and this is how to recognize the end of the foreshots phase. Once the smell of the foreshots is no longer pungent and overpowering it's safe to collect a few drops of distillate on a spoon and taste it.

The point where you switch from the foreshots phase to the heads phase is after the pungent smell and taste of the foreshots have dissipated to the point where they are only faintly detectible. It's not necessary to ensure that the foreshots have completely dissipated before switching to the heads since the heads phase will serve as a buffer to receive the remaining traces of foreshots well before the beginning of the middle-run.

From Table 4 you can see that for a pure-ethanol run with 27L of 95% alcohol you can expect about 435mL of foreshots.

When the foreshots are only faintly detectable, switch to the heads phase. The heads are very nearly pure alcohol except they are very slightly contaminated with early congeners. Heads would not be poisonous to drink but they would have a noticeable off-flavour that would discourage anyone from wanting to drink them.

Throughout the heads phase, periodically collect a few drops of distillate on a spoon and smell and taste it. After an hour or two you'll notice that the harsh off-flavours are slowly fading away to the point where all you'll be able to smell and taste is clean, sweet, raw ethanol. When it reaches this point, let it run for about another 20 minutes then switch to the middle-run. From Table 4 you can see that for this example you can expect about 1,245mL of heads.

The heads should be stored in a container labeled "Redistill" to be processed in a future pure-ethanol distillation.

The run is now in the middle-run phase. The flow rate should be increased slightly to about 12mL per minute. As can be seen from Table 1 this phase ran for close to 31 hours in this example. You should now determine approximately when the middle-run is going to end based on the flow rate and the data you have in your spirit-run record. The run requires very little attention at this stage, all you really need to do is place a large receiver under the output of the still, such as a 19L (5 US gallon) carboy, and check on it every eight to twelve hours until you are within two or three hours of when you've estimated that the middle-run will end.

Each time you check on it, you should note the time, measure the amount of distillate in the receiver and transfer the contents to a collector container, and check the flow rate to make sure that it's staying roughly around 12mL per minute. Small variations are to be expected. Be sure to record your observations in the spirit-run record.

As you get close to the estimated end of the middle-run, begin emptying the receiver frequently because when the tails finally come, the entire contents of the receiver at that time will be contaminated with tails and have to be relegated to the tails phase.

When the end of the middle-run is close, it's useful to begin emptying the contents of the receiver into another container other than the one that you've been collecting the rest of the middle-run in. This is because you want the last ¾L, or more, of middle-run to be relegated to the tails since trace amounts of tail congeners will begin to pervade into the last of the middle-run. This last bit of the middle-run serves as a tails buffer before the tails phase begins. If you emptied say 800mL of middle-run into the main middle-run collector and then the tails came in the next 150mL then the middle-run would only have a 150mL tails buffer. If the 800mL from the last time the receiver was emptied were temporarily kept in a separate container from the main middle-run collector then it could be relegated to the tails, and the tails buffer would be a total of 950mL.

The onset of the tails will be observed by an increase in stillhead temperature. Even a tiny increase from the constant temperature that was observed throughout the middle-run marks the onset of the tails, and therefore the end of the middle-run. The onset of the tails can also be determined by a sudden change in the flavour of the distillate that corresponds to the temperature increase.

There's no need to be concerned about relegating a little more distillate to the heads or tails phases because in the end nothing is lost. The heads and tails are stored as redistil and their alcohol is recovered in the next pure-ethanol run. So, it's best to err on the side of too much heads and tails rather than too little and risk off-flavours in the middle-run.

The tails phase is typically run until the stillhead temperature is about 81 or 82°C (177.5 or 179.5°F). The reason to end it early like this is to avoid accumulating the late congeners in the tails, which are going to be relegated to the redistill. The idea being to keep the redistil as clean as possible so as to minimize the amount of congeners to contend with in the next pure-ethanol run.

However, if you wanted to maximize the amount of ethanol recovered from the run, you could run the tails until the stillhead temperature was 98°C (208.5°F).

The tails should be mixed with the heads in the container labeled "Redistill". In a pure-ethanol distillation the heads and tails are fairly clean and make very good redistil material.

When the ethanol run is complete the packing in the column will be flooded with tails and should be rinsed with hot water. The boiler should be drained and flushed and the still should be thoroughly cleaned out and rinsed as done before in preparation for the run.

The middle-run is the pure ethanol. As mentioned above, it will really only be about 96% ethanol because of the azeotrope it forms with water.

The foreshots should be discarded because they contain almost all of the trace volatile congeners such as acetone, methanol, aldehydes, and esters, which are not potable and should be considered poisonous. With this understanding they can be saved and used as a solvent for paint brushes or oils, or it can be used as gas-line antifreeze. Since it's mostly ethanol, it's very flammable and can be used for things such as barbeque starter. But most importantly, it must not be consumed.

In the *Phase* column of Table 1 there are four phases indicated: **E** for Equilibration; **H** for Heads; **MR** for Middle-Run; and, **T** for Tails.

Actual data from a pure-ethanol run of 36.5L of 70% redistil (1500W)

TIME	Rate of flow (ml/min)	PHASE	Amount Collected (ml)	Amount Collected (Corrected to 100% alc)	Amount Left (ml of 100% alc/vol)	Stillhead Temp °C	% Alcohol of Emerging Distillate	% Alcohol of Aggregate
07:35	0	Start	0		**26,895**	78.5		
09:55	0	Boil	0		26,895	78.5		
10:55	10	E	0		26,895	78.5		
11:25	10	F	250		26,645	78.5	95+	
11:45	10	F	185		26,460	78.5	95+	
13:40	8.5	H	975		25,485	78.5	95+	
14:15	7.7	H	270		25,215	78.5	95+	
18:30	11	MR	2,820		22,395	78.5	95+	
23:35	13.5	MR	4,100		18,295	78.5	95+	
07:40	12.5	MR	6,100		12,195	78.5	95+	
13:30	12.1	MR	4,250		7,945	78.5	95+	
16:30	13.0	MR	2,350		5,595	78.5	95+	
21:00	12.1	MR	3,270		2,325	78.5	95+	
23:00	12.5	T	**1,340***		985	81.2	80	85
23:00		End						

Table 4

* 1,500mL @ 85% corrected to **1,340**mL @ 95% (ie. 1,500 x .85 / .95 = 1,340)

Foreshots (F) :   435mL
Heads (H) : 1,245mL
Middle Run (MR) : 22,890mL
Tails (T) : 1,340mL
Lost :   985mL

Actual Run Time : 36 hours 5 minutes
Estimated Run Time : 37 hours 20 minutes

As for the 985mL recorded as lost, most of that is left in the still. The still was powered down when the head temperature was 81.2°C. If the tails were run until the head temperature was 97 or 98°C and the percent ethanol of the emerging distillate was down to below 20% then the amount lost would be much lower.

However, since the tails are typically relegated to the next collection of redistill, most distillers prefer to avoid accumulating all the late congeners that are received during the last part of the tails phase and sacrifice some of the alcohol to produce cleaner tails to be put in the next redistill.

Diluting: There are many uses for pure ethanol but most involve dilution to drinking strength (ie. 40 to 50% abv). For vodka, gin and most essence-based spirits, dilution to drinking strength is all that's required, but for some liqueurs that have a large amount of ingredients that would further dilute the spirit it may be necessary to start out with a higher concentration of ethanol in order to end up with the desired drinking strength.

It's best to use soft or pure water for dilution. Hard water should be avoided because, not only can it impart off flavours, but it can cast a white precipitate that often results in a turbid or cloudy appearance, or a chalky sediment at the bottom of the bottle. This precipitate is perfectly harmless, but is aesthetically unpleasing.

A formula to use for calculating the amount of water needed to dilute the middle-run (MR) to the desired percent ethanol is as follows:

Vol of MR x % alc of MR / (Desired % alc - Vol of MR) = Vol of water required

eg. 22,890ml x 95% / (40% - 22,890ml) = 31,470ml

After dilution this would produce 54.36L of 40% abv.

Storage: Distilled spirits should be stored in glass, not plastic. Although vodka, gin, and other colourless spirits do not require aging, they do improve for up to five weeks after being made. Even commercial producers of these spirits ensure their product is not shipped for about three months after bottling.

OTHER WHISKEY-MASH RECIPES

In *Chapter 6 Mashing* a recipe was given for an all-grain corn mash. This recipe was a pure corn whiskey recipe that complied with US Government standards for commercial whiskey production. Further to this, the recipe was modeled after modern commercial whiskey making methods. It employed scientific means of ensuring very high quality and efficient grain extraction.

However, there are many other whiskey recipes. Some are employed by commercial whiskey distilleries, others are only of interest to hobbyists and home distillers, and others remain traditional old folk recipes that are beginning to attract the attention of home- and micro-distilleries.

The following are some of the recipes that the author has experimented with and had excellent results.

THIN-MASH RECIPE

The thin-mash recipe is probably the most common whiskey recipe among home and small-scale distillers. Commercial distillers do not generally adopt this type of recipe because it doesn't comply with US Government standards for the definition of whiskey. Under US law, as well as under the laws of most other whiskey-producing nations, a spirit must be made with all grain (among other requirements) in order to be allowed to carry the name "whiskey". Thin-mash recipes contain sugar and are therefore not all-grain recipes.

Although the thin-mash recipe described below is for corn mash, this process applies equally to all other forms of grain mash such as rye, bourbon, malt, millet, etc.

Contrary to what purists say, many people find that thin-mash recipes produce excellent-tasting whiskey, and some contend that they prefer it to all-grain recipes.

The best way to make a thin mash is to make up a batch of all-grain corn mash as described in *Chapter 6 Mashing*, but rather than chilling the mash simply place an equal volume of cold water in a fermenter and add the hot mash to the cold water. This dilutes the corn mash 50/50, hence the name "thin mash". It also cools it to yeast-pitching temperature (ie. below 38°C (100°F)). As well as cooling the mashing, this dilution eliminates the need to oxygenate it. The cold water will contain ample oxygen for yeast growth.

If an entire 30L batch of all-grain mash were made, as per the recipe in *Chapter 6 Mashing*, the total volume after dilution would be 60L. Even after straining, this would be too large a batch size for a single beer-stripping run in the spirit still detailed in *Chapter 4 Equipment*. So, you can either make a half batch or, preferably, remove half of a full batch and freeze it for future use and simply make up the other half to give a 30L batch of thin mash.

Once the mash is diluted, the sugar concentration will need to be restored back to the original Starting Gravity (SG) of between 1.060 and 1.070. For a 30L batch of thin mash, add 4.5L (4.5Kg) of corn sugar. Corn sugar (ie. dextrose) gives a smoother flavour than regular table sugar (ie. sucrose), but table sugar is widely used in thin mashes and gives very good results. Because sucrose has more sugar molecules per kilogram than dextrose, you only need to add 3.6L (3.6Kg) of table sugar to achieve the same SG as 4.5L (4.5Kg) of dextrose.

Ensuring the temperature is below 38°C (100°F) and the SG is between 1.060 and 1.070, the same type and quantity of yeast and enzyme as used in *Chapter 7 Fermentation* can be added.

From this point on the thin mash can be fermented, strained, and distilled in the same manner as the all-grain recipe. However, the fermentation will typically take a day or so longer.

In this recipe the thin mash was made up of 50% corn mash and 50% sugar and water. In practice, many distillers dilute the mash even more with sugar and water. For example, 25% corn mash and 75% sugar and water. Or, even 10% corn and 90% sugar and water. Keep in mind that further dilution requires proportionally more sugar. In the case of the 25/75 ratio, the sugar addition would be

6.75L (6.75Kg) of corn sugar rather than the 4.5L (4.5Kg) used in the 50/50 ratio.

If the mash is diluted more than 50/50, fermentation becomes a problem. Grain mash provides certain essential nutrients for the yeast that are not present in straight sugar and water. So, thin mashes that are "too thin" have difficulty fermenting without the addition of chemical nutrients, which can alter the flavour.

It is recommended that a thin mash not be diluted to more than 25/75, and for anything under 50/50, fermentation times will be noticeably longer.

If low mash ratios are desired for some reason, it will be necessary to use nutrients. An obvious way for a home distiller to do this would be to use turbo yeast. However, the yeast strains used in turbo yeasts are not generally chosen for their suitability for making whiskey, so the flavour profile of the whiskey produced would not likely be good.

If it's possible to buy the turbo-yeast nutrients without the yeast, then a nutrient pack could be used in conjunction with a proper whiskey yeast strain. Notwithstanding this, an addition of 50gmof diammonium phosphate per 25 to 30L of mash will help the fermentation considerably.

MASHING WITH BACKSET

"Backset" is the clear residue left in the still boiler after a beer-stripping run is completed. Normally, one just flushes this residue away as the waste left over after the mash is distilled. However, backset can make a remarkable contribution to the flavour of a subsequent batch of whiskey.

Backset has a comparatively low pH, typically around 3.3, and is quite sour. In fact, it's backset that makes sour mash sour. Sour mash will be discussed later in *Chapter 13 Traditional Sour-Mash Whiskey*.

In a regular grain-mash recipe, backset can be used to lower the pH of the mash water to 6.0. For example, the pH of 23L of a typical tap-water with 2 tsp of gypsum can be lowered from a pH of about 9.0 to 6.0 by the addition of about 400mL of backset. Of course, different starting pHs will require different amounts of backset. Using backset also eliminates the need for handling strong acids to do the pH adjustment.

Because of its lubricious effect on the whiskey flavour, some distillers are motivated to add more backset than the relatively small amount required to lower the pH to 6.0. This can't really be done to any significant extent because the malt enzymes can only tolerate a pH as low as about 4.6, lower than that will denature the malt enzymes.

If you do use more backset remember that the addition of the grain to the mash water will further lower the pH, and also keep in mind that the malt enzymes will be functioning below their optimum pH range.

Backset that is being saved for future mashings should be collected in plastic 4L (1 gallon) jugs and frozen until required. Backset is quite susceptible to bacterial contamination so it should be kept frozen between uses. It's also very easy for a whiskey distiller to get backset, so it's usually not necessary to store much of it at a time.

After the mash water has been prepared with backset, the procedure is the same as described in *Chapter 6 Mashing* and *Chapter 7 Fermentation* for making and fermenting the mash.

ALL-GRAIN MALT-WHISKEY RECIPE

Malt whiskey is the whiskey style that scotch whisky falls into. Basically, scotch is an all-grain malt whiskey made entirely of 2-row barley malt and water. Scotch whisky (ie. malt whiskey made in Scotland) generally has other elements contributing to its flavour, such as the smoky, peaty flavour that comes from barley malt that was kilned over a peat fire and water from a natural source that contains peat and heather characteristics that are imparted from the ground it flows from. However, Lowland scotches have very little of these characteristics, as do malt whiskies from parts of the world other than Scotland, and these malt whiskies are excellent in their own right.

Unlike corn or rye mash, malt mash is not fermented with the grain still in the mash. The grain in a malt mash is strained out and rinsed before fermentation, much the same as how beer is made.

Malt mash is made just like an all-grain beer except there are no hops and no kettle boil. However, since there's no kettle boil, sparging, a process usually employed when making beer (ie. a method of straining and rinsing the grain with hot water), runs the risk of over diluting the mash, so rinsing the grain must be handled carefully. One precaution would be to limit the over-all amount of mash water that's used in the entire mash cycle.

The following is a single infusion-mash method for making an all-grain malt mash.

One consideration when making a malt-whiskey mash is that a whiskey mash typically has an originating SG between 1.060 and 1.070. This is a little difficult to achieve with a straight infusion mash with no kettle boil, so this recipe is formulated to yield a SG of 1.060 or a little higher, based on a modest mash-extract efficiency of about 72%.

Mash-extract efficiency is a measure of how well the brewing operation extracts the carbohydrates from the grain and renders them to the finished substrate for fermentation. Ideally, a brewing operation would extract 100% of the carbohydrates from the grain, but various inefficiencies in the process, such as rinsing the grain, result in some of them remaining in the spent grain.

Naturally, home operations tend not to be as efficient as commercial operations, so the modest mash-extract efficiency of 72% has been assumed for the formulation of this recipe.

Equipment

> 34-40L pot with lid
> smaller pot (6 to 8L) with lid
> strainer or straining bag
> a large plastic or wooden stirring spoon
> a floating dairy thermometer, graduated from 0°C to 110°C (32°F to 230°F)
> pH papers, range 5.0-6.5; or pH meter
> pH papers, range 2-12; or pH meter
> tincture of iodine
> measuring spoons
> eye dropper

Ingredients

> 25L of fairly soft municipal tap water, eg. hardness level of 4; almost no iron; 100 ppm calcium; pH 8.5.
> 10mL (2-tsp) Gypsum ($CaSO_4$)
> 95% sulphuric acid (H_2SO_4); or, citric or tartaric acid; or backset
> 6.6Kg (14.5 lbs) crushed 2-row pale barley malt
> 60gm(1/3 cup) active dried distillers' yeast plus 1 tsp distillery glucoamylase
> Or
> 1 package of whiskey yeast/enzyme combination

Method

Prepare 25L of mash water by thoroughly mixing 10mL (2-tsp) of gypsum into the water and adjust the pH to about 6.0 with acid or backset.

Place 17L of the mash water in the large pot, set it on the stove, and turn the stove on high. Cover the pot, and let the water heat up to the conversion strike temperature of 71°C (160°F). Periodically, you will have to stir the water thoroughly and check the temperature as the water heats up until the strike temperature is reached.

When the water is at the strike temperature, turn off the heat, and stir in the 6.6Kg (14.5 lbs) of barley malt. The temperature should come

Chapter 12 Other Whiskey-Mash Recipes

to rest at about 65.5°C (150°F) or higher. Stir the mash for about five minutes.

Cover the mash pot and leave it for 90 minutes for the starches to convert to sugars. It's helpful to stir the mash every 15 minutes or so during this conversion rest. The temperature will start out around 65.5°C (150°F) and will drop to about 60°C (140°F) throughout the 90-minutes. This is just about right since the ideal conversion temperature is about 62.5°C (145°F), which is about midway between the starting and ending temperatures.

Towards the end of the conversion rest, place 4L of mash water in the smaller pot and heat it almost to boil. This will be used shortly after the conversion rest is complete.

After the 90-minute conversion rest, the starches should be completely converted to sugars. This can be tested for by the iodine starch test.

Next the mash must be strained into a fermenter using a strainer or a straining bag. After this, return all the grain from the strainer or straining bag to the mash pot, and add the 4L of hot water from the smaller pot. Mix the grains thoroughly in the hot water, and strain it again into the fermenter. Return the grain to the mash pot again and repeat this rinsing process once more with another 4L of near-boiling mash water.

Once the grain has been strained and rinsed into the fermenter, the mash should be chilled to yeast-pitching temperature (ie. under 38°C (100°F)) with an immersion chiller.

People with homebrewing sparging equipment can adapt this procedure to employ all-grain brewing methods of mashing and sparging, but they must take care not to use more than a total of 25L of mash water and sparge water, or the SG of the mash will be lower than desired (ie. less than 1.060). So, the amount of sparge water must be kept to a minimum.

A SG of less than 1.060 will work okay, but the yield per gallon will be less.

From this point on the mash can be fermented and distilled in the usual manner. Since the mash has already been strained it won't require straining after fermentation, but it must be carefully siphoned off its yeast sediment before transferring to the still.

Malt whiskies lend themselves very well to oak aging. They can either be aged in new charred oak barrels in the American straight-whiskey style, or they can be aged in used barrels as in the Scottish, Irish, and Canadian styles.

MALT-EXTRACT RECIPES

Unhopped pale malt extract, as sold in homebrew shops, can be used to make an excellent mash for a malt whiskey. And, it's very convenient, one only needs to reconstitute the malt extract with water to a SG between 1.060 and 1.070, and add yeast and enzyme as described in *Chapter 7 Fermentation*.

Dried Malt Extract (DME) tends to yield a better flavour than malt-extract syrups. The malt-extract syrups produce whiskey that has a stewed or cooked flavour that just isn't true to style. This flavour is not all that bad, and many people enjoy it, but it just isn't consistent with what is expected in a malt whiskey. DME, on the other hand, doesn't impart this cooked flavour.

This same difference is also observed in beers made with malt extract. Beer made with extract syrups tends to have a cooked or caramel flavour that works very well in the rich dark ales, but is generally unwanted in light lagers. DME is very well suited to making the lighter beers and doesn't confer that cooked or caramel flavour to them.

The reason for this cooked flavour in malt-extract syrups is because of the way the syrups are made. Malt-extract syrup is made by taking a regular all-grain brewers wort made from fresh malted barley, and evaporating the water from it until it has the consistency of a syrup. The water is evaporated from the wort using equipment similar to that used to make freeze-dried or cold-evaporated instant coffee, however some boiling is involved and that is what results in the cooked character of the flavour.

DME is made by taking the fresh wort and spraying it against a stainless steel mesh in a chamber where hot dried air is passing through. This dries the wort to a solid on the mesh without having to boil it. Therefore, the DME doesn't have the cooked flavour.

An all-malt-extract whiskey can be made by placing 4.5Kg (10 lbs) of unhopped pale malt-extract syrup or 3.8Kg (8 1/3 lbs) of light DME in a fermenter, and then top up to 20L with warm water to give 20L of mash at 38°C (100°F) and a SG of about 1.070.

The mash can then be fermented with whiskey yeast and enzyme as explained in *Chapter 7 Fermentation*. This type of mash has no suspended solids the way a grain recipe does, so there's no need to strain the mash after the fermentation, but it will require careful siphoning off the yeast sediment before transferring to the still.

The fermentation will take about a day or two longer than an all-grain recipe, and is distilled in the same manner as other whiskey mashes.

Like all-grain malt whiskies, malt-extract whiskies lend themselves very well to oak aging.

THIN MALT-EXTRACT RECIPES

Malt-extract whiskies can also be made as thin-mash recipes by diluting with sugar and water. And, like other thin-mash recipes they work out very well.

A thin malt-extract mash can be made by placing 2.6Kg (5.75 lbs) of unhopped pale malt-extract syrup, or 2.2Kg (4.85 lbs) of light DME, and 2Kg (4.4 lbs) of corn sugar in a fermenter, and then top up to 20L with warm water to give 20L of mash at 38°C (100°F) and a SG of about 1.070.

The fermentation and distillation are done the same way as for the all-malt-extract recipes. The higher proportion of sugar and lower proportion of extract will mean slightly longer fermentation times.

WHEAT MALT-EXTRACT RECIPES

Wheat-malt extract is excellently suited to making whiskey, and also works very well as an adjunct to grain mashes. Some distillers contend that wheat-malt extract is much more suited to making whiskey than the standard barley-malt extract.

Wheat contributes flavour attributes to whiskey that are very similar to those of rye. In fact, at least one commercial bourbon distillery uses wheat in place of rye for their world-famous bourbon.

One could make a wheat-malt extract whiskey by either the all-malt-extract or thin-malt-extract recipes above, the procedures are the same. Or, wheat malt could be used as an adjunct to a straight corn mash recipe.

An excellent bourbon mash can be made by taking a straight all-grain corn mash, as detailed in *Chapter 6 Mashing*, and then diluting it by adding about 1/3 its volume in water (roughly 10L), and then mixing in 2Kg (4.4 lbs) of light dried wheat malt extract to give a mash with a SG of about 1.065 to 1.070. The mash is then fermented and distilled in the usual manner.

PEAT-SMOKED MALT RECIPES

Scotch whisky is world famous for its signature peat-smoke flavour. The peat-smoke flavour comes from drying the barley malt over peat fires. The malt kilns are designed in a manner that allows the smoke from the peat fire under the kiln to enter the malt chamber and impregnate the malt with the smoke from the burning peat.

The peat-smoke flavour is not to be confused with the peat flavour, which scotch is also notorious for. The peat flavour actually comes from the spring water that the scotch is made from. The spring water flows over a lot of peat (ie. a precursor to coal that's very abundant in Scotland) and it picks up the peat flavour that pervades into the finished scotch.

The barley malt that is generally available in homebrew shops is not kilned over open peat fires, and therefore does not impart this characteristic peat-smoke flavour to malt whiskey. However, a lot of homebrew shops carry peat-smoked malt as a specialty grain to be used in Scottish ales. These peat-smoked specialty malts have a very high degree of peat smoke to them and could never be used alone to produce a malt whiskey. In fact, most distillers who experiment with peat-smoked specialty malt usually settle on about 6 to 8 ounces (170 to 230 g) in the formulation of a 25L malt-mash recipe.

In the case of an all-grain malt mash, the peat-smoked malt can simply be combined with the rest of the malt in the recipe and the mash procedure can be carried out as usual.

In the case of a malt-extract mash, the peat-smoked malt should be placed in a boiling bag (ie. a cheese-cloth-like bag available at homebrew shops for boiling hops or steeping specialty grains) and steeped in about 4L of 65.5°C (150°F) mash water for about 30 minutes, then removed and discarded. The 4L of mash water is then incorporated in the rest of the mash water for the recipe.

Some marbles or a shot glass should be placed in the boiling bag with the peat-smoked malt in order to weight it down and keep it immersed in the water. Also, the peat-smoked malt should be very loosely packed in the boiling bag so the hot water can freely pass through the bag and come into maximum contact with the grain.

Another method of doing this is to steep the peat-smoked malt directly in the 4L of mash water without the boiling bag, but the grains will require straining out after.

The amount of peat-smoked malt that any particular distiller will decide upon is subject to personal preference, and can be adjusted up or down from batch to batch until the preferred amount is determined, but one approach that can be taken is to make up a batch of straight peat-smoked malt whiskey and then blend it with plain malt whiskey. This enables the distiller to blend to a much more exacting level of smokiness.

Before doing a straight all-grain peat-smoke mash, it's important to ensure that the peat-smoked malt still has a reasonable level of diastatic enzymes present in it. Specialty malts are often kilned to very high temperatures, thereby destroying their diastatic enzymes.

This is normally not a problem in beer brewing because the specialty malts are typically only small adjuncts to the recipe and are not intended to supply the bulk of the enzymes. So, it's best to confirm with the supplier as to the enzyme level of the peat-smoked malt.

If you are unable to find peat-smoked malt with a sufficient enzyme level, you can make up a batch of malt whiskey with a fairly large amount of peat-smoked malt, say 1Kg (2.2 lbs). That will produce a whiskey with a very high amount of peat-smoke flavour that can be used to blend with.

BOURBON-MASH RECIPES

The basic-bourbon mash recipe is identical to the pure-corn-whiskey recipe detailed in *Chapter 6 Mashing*, with the exception that the grain bill is comprised of 5 parts corn and 3 parts rye, rather than just straight corn. Different distillers will use different proportions of corn and rye, but 5 parts corn and 3 parts rye is a fairly common mix. The adjunct of barley malt remains unchanged, as does the rest of the recipe.

At least one bourbon distillery uses wheat in place of rye with absolutely excellent results. So, a grain bill of 5 parts corn and 3 parts wheat, or 6 parts corn and 2 parts wheat also produces an excellent bourbon mash.

Bourbon mash recipes benefit very well from the addition of backset to the mash water, as explained above. The addition of backset to the mash water for a bourbon recipe is basically the cooked-style of sour mash bourbon. The no-cook style will be discussed in *Chapter 13 Traditional Sour-Mash Whiskey*.

Both flaked rye and flaked wheat are readily available from the same suppliers as flaked maize.

RYE-MASH RECIPES

The rye-mash recipe is basically the same as the bourbon-mash recipe, except the proportions in the grain bill are reversed. For example, 5 parts rye and 3 parts corn, or 6 parts rye and 2 parts corn.

Chapter 12 Other Whiskey-Mash Recipes 141

Other cereal grains such as wheat can be used in place of corn, but rye distillers are more likely to go with straight rye rather than recipes calling for other grains. In fact, some rye distillers insist on 100% rye, including the malt. They use rye malt instead of barley malt so that the mash is comprised entirely of rye.

Rye malt is available at homebrew shops as a specialty malt, and it has a very high diastatic enzyme count that's similar to that of 6-row barley malt, so rye malt is very well suited to making whiskey mash in general and is worth experimenting with for other recipes as well as 100% rye whiskey.

Rye has an interesting property to it in that straight un-malted rye grain contains alpha-amylase enzymes. These are the enzymes that "liquefy" the mash. The liquefaction phase of the mash cycle is the phase where the long-chain insoluble starches, which make the mash thick like a porridge, are reduced to short-chain soluble starches, hence liquefying the mash. These enzymes can be activated by a mash rest at 65 - 70°C (149 - 158°F).

In practice, it's a little difficult to exploit these enzymes, and somewhat unnecessary since there's ample enzymes in the malt to do the entire mash conversion. However, if you're mashing flaked rye then the initial rest at 68°C (155°F), after the flaked rye is added to the 74°C (165°F) mash water, will effect a liquefaction rest during the period before the malt is added. This rest is not at all important to the mash cycle but it does give the malt enzymes a good head start.

If you're mashing non-flaked rye such as rye flour or rye meal, which requires infusion into the mash water at near boiling temperatures and then a rest for 10 or 15 minutes to disperse the starches, then this liquefaction rest becomes impractical. The near-boiling temperatures would denature the enzymes, so they would not be active by the time the mash cooled to 68°C (155°F). However, commercial distilleries do take advantage of these enzymes when mashing rye because they can actually reduce the over-all amount of energy used in the process.

In order to use these enzymes when mashing non-flaked rye they have to employ a step-mash regimen rather than doing a straight infusion mash. To do a step-mash procedure, the grain must be added to 74°C (165°F) mash water for a 10 or 15-minute rest at 68°C (155°F) until the mash liquefies. Next the mash temperature must be raised to near-boiling temperatures by either applying heat while vigorously agitating, or by additions of boiling mash water. The mash is left to rest at the higher temperature for 10 or 15 minutes to disperse.

The mash is then either chilled or left to cool to 66.5°C (152°F) and the malt is added. The process is the same as for the other methods from here on.

It's unlikely that a home operation would realize any energy savings by employing this method, and it would certainly be a lot more trouble and time consuming than doing a straight infusion mash. So, it's recommended that if you're mashing non-flaked rye that you ignore the indigenous alpha-amylase enzymes in the rye and conduct the mash cycle in the same manner as with any other grain.

CORN-SQUEEZINS' WHISKEY

Corn squeezins' is the juice that flows from a corn silo when it's being filled with corn cobs or silage. Invariably each farmer would have his/her own way of catching the corn squeezins' from their corn silos, but one popular method was to place a dozen or more clay crocks with their lids in place but ajar slightly on the floor of the silo just before the corn was blown into it at harvest time.

They'd leave the crocks there all winter and retrieve them in the spring, and the crocks would be full to the brim with corn squeezins', completely and naturally fermented, and ready to distill.

This makes a surprisingly pleasant corn whiskey, it has a kind of natural grassy taste to it, but it tends to be well liked, and it has a strong and distinct corn-whiskey flavour.

It would follow that if a more systematic means were devised to collect the juice and a proper whiskey yeast were used, the flavour and the yield would be significantly improved. A lot of juice is produced when a corn silo is being filled, so if a system were devised to collect it all, it would produce a very generous yield.

Unfortunately, corn squeezins' is not something you can buy or make, either you live on a farm with a corn silo or you don't. Some people may know a farmer who would let them harvest their corn squeezins', but notwithstanding that, there's no real way get corn squeezins'.

Now, a close approximation can be made by taking fresh corn right off the cob and squeezing the juice from it. This juice can be fermented with a whiskey yeast and then distilled. It'll make a good whiskey, but it won't be exactly the same as the corn squeezins' whiskey. The reason for this is that the corn squeezins' contains a lot of juice from the stocks as well as the corn itself.

Some farmers swear by this method of making corn whiskey as yielding the very best flavour of all the methods of preparing and fermenting corn. This is consistent with the view that some distillers have that the no-cook corn-mash methods make the best whiskey, such as the sour-mash whiskey method detailed in *Chapter 13 Traditional Sour-Mash Whiskey*. Their flavour is more natural and the flavour of the corn (or other grain) pervades very well into the finished spirit. And, there's no doubt that the corn-squeezins' method is definitely a no-cook recipe.

CHAPTER 13

TRADITIONAL SOUR-MASH WHISKEY

The mash recipe discussed in *Chapter 6 Mashing* is a cooker-mash style that involves heating the grain and the water to specific temperatures and then introducing malt enzymes to effect a complete conversion of the starches to sugars. This chapter details the traditional no-cook sour-mash style of mash.

Both the cooker-mash method and the sour-mash method produce their own distinctive flavour characteristics, complete with their proponents who prefer one over the other.

PRINCIPLES

The cooker-mash method produces a mash where all the grain starches are efficiently and completely converted to sugars, which are then converted to alcohol in a single fermentation.

The principle behind the no-cook sour-mash method is to ferment raw grain and sugar in pH-adjusted water. In a pH-optimized substrate, yeast will secrete enzymes that break grain starches down to sugars.

However, this no-cook process is inherently inefficient, only about 30%, at best, of the grain starches are actually consumed during the fermentation. For this reason, the used grain and the backset from one batch are carried over to the next. The "backset" is the spent liquid left in the still boiler after a beer-stripping run is finished. This process of recycling ingredients from one batch to the next is called "mashing back".

The practice of repeatedly mashing back compensates for this inefficiency. A single quantity of grain is cycled through three fermentations before it's discarded.

Mashing back not only recovers the unused grain starches and sugars left over from a prior batch, but it produces the distinctive flavour characterized by sour mashing.

The flavour of whiskey produced by the cooker-mash method has a pleasant and refined nature that's typical of commercially produced whiskey.

Whiskey produced by the sour-mash method has a more natural taste that more-closely resembles the flavour of the grain itself. People say they can actually taste the corn or the rye in the whiskey.

Although both methods, the cooker-mash and the sour-mash, are quite straightforward and easy to follow, the sour-mash method is operationally simpler and easier to implement. For this reason, a novice distiller may want to start out with this method and move to the cooker-mash method later when they're more familiar with the overall procedures of mashing, fermenting, and distilling.

The traditional sour-mash method is simple and unscientific, and is functionally inefficient. However, the practice of mashing back is quite ingenious and very little is actually lost in the process.

Being a no-cook mashing method, with sour mash the raw grain and mash water are mixed at fermentation temperature, sugar and yeast are added, and the mash is fermented without any cooking.

In order for this method to work, the pH of the mash should at least be between 3.0 and 6.0, and optimally between 4.5 and 5.5. The pH is crucial to the function of this method. The sugar gets the yeast started but then the yeast begins breaking down the grain starches to sugars. It also breaks down some of the grain proteins into amino acids, which serve as a nutrient to the yeast. But, all this depends on the pH being within the acceptable range.

It was because of this dependency on a suitable pH that the old-time distillers always insisted that the water had to be suited to whiskey making or it wouldn't work. Although it's unlikely the old-time distillers knew about pH, they did discover telltale signs as to whether a source water was suitable or not. They would look for certain plants or wild flowers growing along side the brooks, streams, or lakes. And, they would avoid water sources that had certain other plants or flowers growing along side them. This presence or absence of certain flora gave clues to the water chemistry of the source water, which would include pH.

One method that was fashionable for a long time was the Ivory Soap test. Ivory Soap, unlike most other soaps, was very nearly pure soap (ie. "99.44% pure") and didn't contain water-softening compounds in its formulation to aid in its use in hard water. The distillers, casing out a new source water, would mix some of the water with Ivory Soap. If it easily produced a good lather, they would conclude that the water was good for making whiskey. Now, if pure soap (ie. soap devoid of water-softening compounds) raises a good lather in a sample of source water then that indicates the water is soft. Pure soap won't raise a good lather in hard water. Soft water is most likely to have a pH of about 7.0 (ie. the pH of pure water), which is within the range of suitable pH for sour mash considering that the addition of the grain to the water further lowers the pH. So, a mash water with pH 7.0 will have a pH of about 6.0 after the grain is added.

This, of course, is not within the optimum pH range of 4.5 to 5.5, but it is workable. As will be seen below, the pH of the mash will decrease significantly during the fermentation, and the backset that it turns into will supply ample acid to the subsequent sour-mash cycle.

As mentioned above, the yeast enzymes in this method will only consume about 30% of the grain starches, at best, but the uptake of the sugar added will be very good.

When the fermentation is complete, the liquid part of the mash is removed and distilled. The backset from that distillation is cooled and returned to the grain in the fermenter (ie. mashed back), more source water and sugar are added, and a second fermentation is conducted on the same grain. This can be repeated two or three times on the same batch of grain. There's no need to add yeast to the subsequent batches because there's ample yeast left in the grain.

Both the grain and the backset carried over to the subsequent batches are very sour, so it becomes quite clear how the name "sour mash" originated.

The practice of mashing back not only recuperates residual starches in the grain and unfermented sugar in the backset, but it even retains residual alcohol left in the backset to be recycled through the next batch. Distillers are even known to leverage this fact and deliberately leave the last 15 or 20% of the alcohol in the still to save on energy and time. The last 15% of the alcohol in a batch requires the most energy and takes the longest to recover since the percent alcohol of the flowing distillate at that point is down to below 20% and decreasing. By ending the run early the residual alcohol is simply carried over to the next batch, and energy is saved.

The backset has a pH of about 3.3 and the used grain, with its standing liquid, has a similar pH. This is considerably below the optimum range of 4.5 and 5.5. Even the addition of some comparatively high-pH source water (eg. 8.5) doesn't help much to raise the pH, but sour mash will ferment surprisingly well under these conditions.

It may occur to some distillers to try and raise the pH of the sour mash by the addition of calcium hydroxide (lime) or calcium carbonate (precipitated chalk) but the amount required to raise the pH to the optimum level is much too high to serve as a sustainable means of controlling sour-mash pH.

Nevertheless, sour mash ferments just fine with its low pH, so no action needs to be taken to adjust it.

PROCEDURE

This section describes how to make 30L (32 US quarts) of no-cook sour mash[‡], 20 – 25L (21 – 26 US quarts) to be distilled after straining. As discussed above, sour mashing is an iterative process, and two methods will be detailed here: "the intermittent sour-mash cycle"; and, "the continuous sour-mash cycle".

[‡] The sour-mash methods described in this section were adapted from, *Simple Sour Mash to Simple Alcohol Fuel*, by J. W. Walstad, of the Revenoor Stills Co., Ltd. www.revenoor.com.

Equipment

34 – 40L (36 – 42 US quarts) fermenter with lid (a mash pot of the same size will work very well)
a heating pad
a large plastic or wooden stirring spoon
a pH meter, or pH papers: range 5.0 – 6.5 & 3.0 – 4.5
a floating dairy thermometer, graduated from 0 to 110°C (32 to 230°F)
a wine & beer hydrometer
3 plastic pails: 20 – 25L (21 – 26 US quarts)
eye dropper

Ingredients

25L (26 US quarts) of fairly soft municipal tap water, eg. hardness level of 4; almost no iron; 100 ppm calcium; pH 8.5.
10ml (2 tsp) Gypsum ($CaSO_4$)
95% sulphuric acid (H_2SO_4); or citric or tartaric acid; or about 400ml of backset
4.55Kg (10 lbs) of grain meal (eg. corn meal, rye meal, millet meal)
2.75Kg (6 lbs) of table sugar (sucrose); or, 3.4Kg (7.5 lbs) of corn sugar (dextrose)
1.5L of whiskey-yeast starter; or, ¼ cup (45gm) of active dried whiskey yeast
Or
1 package of whiskey yeast/enzyme combination

Method 1 – Intermittent Sour-Mash Cycle

In an intermittent sour-mash cycle, three batches of mash are produced from a single quantity of grain. The grain is then discarded, and the cycle is repeated with new grain. The process is intermittent in that it begins, ends, and must be started over, as opposed to a continuous cycle that can be propagated indefinitely.

For most home distillers the intermittent cycle is the most suitable because it requires less attention and they don't typically want to do more than three or six iterations at a time.

1ˢᵗ Batch

If you are using a 1.5L whiskey-yeast starter, make sure it's fermenting and ready to pitch before proceeding to the next steps.

Prepare the mash water in a separate container from the fermentation vessel (eg. a 25L pail). Place 25L (26 US quarts) of 30°C (85°F) tap water in the container and thoroughly mix the 10ml (2-tsp) of gypsum into the water. Measure the pH and adjust it to about 6.0 using acid or backset.

Place the 4.55Kg (10 lbs) of grain in the fermenter and add 5L (5 US quarts) of mash water to wet and cover the grain. Mix thoroughly and ensure the grain is completely covered, add more water if required.

Next, add another 20L (21 US quarts) of mash water and mix thoroughly. The idea is to add enough water to cover the grain plus about 20L (21 US quarts).

Add the sugar and mix thoroughly. The S.G. will be about 1.055. Measure the pH, ideally it should be between 4.5 and 5.5 to optimize the uptake of the grain starches. This first batch will most likely be in that range, but it's not a major concern if it's outside by as much as 1.5. It can be as low as 3.0 and still work very well, however, it shouldn't be much above 6.0 at the most.

Add the yeast and mix it in. If using a yeast starter, decant the liquid from the starter and just add the slurry to the mash. If the starter is very active and too much of the slurry is suspended in the liquid, the entire 1.5L starter can be added to the mash without decanting with no real adverse effect.

Place the fermenter squarely on the heating pad, plug it in, and set it at low. Float the hydrometer and the dairy thermometer in the mash. This is where using a mash pot as a fermenter is beneficial. The metal pot conducts the heat from the heating pad into the fermenting mash much more efficiently than a plastic fermenter does.

Over the course of the fermentation, ensure the temperature of the mash stays between 26 and 33°C (80 and 90°F), adjust the heating-pad setting if necessary.

It's very nearly impossible to determine how much alcohol will be produced because the Originating Gravity (OG) will only be a measure of the amount of sugar in the water. Throughout the fermentation the grain starches will be converted to sugars and fermented, so there's an uptake of extract from the grain that's not measurable at the outset of the fermentation.

Since the potential-alcohol calculation is a function of the total extract, not knowing the total extract makes it impossible to calculate the amount of alcohol to expect.

Also, numerous experiments with vinometers and refractometers did not give consistent nor accurate readings of the alcohol content of the mash after the fermentation was complete. So, measuring the alcohol content of the low wines with a proof hydrometer after the beer-stripping run is probably the only economical means of accurately determining the amount of alcohol produced.

The fermentation will be quite vigorous and should take from 60 to 80 hours. The Terminating Gravity (TG) should be well below 1.000 for the first batch.

After the fermentation is complete, remove the liquid from the sedimented grain either by siphoning, or ladling with a measuring cup or small pot, and cover the fermenter. There will be from 20 to 25L (21 to 26 US quarts) of liquid.

Transfer the liquid to the still and do a beer-stripping run on it. After the still cools down and the backset is under 38°C (100°F), remove the backset from the still. The backset will need to be aerated, so a vigorous draining from the still to a container (eg. plastic pail) with a lot of splashing will accomplish this very well. If this is not possible, the backset will have to be aerated in some other manner.

There will typically be 14 to 19L (15 to 20 US quarts) of backset and it will have a pH of roughly 3.3. As mentioned above, this pH is considerably below the optimum range of 4.5 to 5.5, but nevertheless, it will work remarkably well in the next iteration of fermentation.

2nd Batch

Pour the backset into the fermenter with the grain from the first batch, and add another charge of sugar. Top up the fermenter with straight, untreated tap water to the same level as the first batch, this typically requires 5 or 6L (5 or 6 US quarts).

There will be no need to add yeast, the grain will contain ample yeast slurry from the first time around. Keep the fermenter on the heating pad and maintain the fermentation temperature between 26 and 33°C (80 and 90°F).

The fermentation will usually take 10 to 15 hours longer than for the first batch. When the fermentation is complete, remove the liquid and distil it as before. The low wines should be saved and accumulated with the low wines from the first batch.

3rd Batch

As with the first batch, when the backset has cooled to below 38°C (100°F), transfer it to a container, aerate it, and pour it back into the fermenter with the grain. Add another charge of sugar, top it up with tap water, and ferment as with the second batch.

The fermentation will invariably take even longer than the second batch and it may even be incomplete with a TG well above 1.000. This is because the grain has been exhausted and is not contributing as much nutrient to the fermentation. This is not a problem, when the fermentation has stopped, or almost stopped, remove the liquid and distil it, and save the low wines with the low wines from the previous two batches. Any unfermented sugars in the liquid will be recovered when the backset is incorporated in a future sour mash cycle.

After the third iteration, the grain will be spent and should be discarded. Spent grain, laced with active living yeast, makes excellent compost, so if composting is an option for you then this is an excellent way to dispose of the spent grain.

The backset from the third batch can be used in the first iteration of the next sour-mash cycle in place of the mash water. Just use the backset topped up with straight tap water. Don't do any pH adjustment, it will already be very low.

Method 2 – Continuous Sour-Mash Cycle

A continuous sour-mash cycle is formulated exactly the same as an intermittent cycle except the spent grains, which float to the top, are periodically removed with a strainer. As individual grains become spent they turn a slightly darker colour and float to the top of the mash.

For this method, the floating grains must be skimmed from the mash two or three times per day. The spent grains should be kept and accumulated so as to know the total amount removed. Spent grains will only float for about twelve hours and then they sink back down into the sediment. It's important to skim the spent grains while they are floating because after they sink there will be no way to separate them from the unspent grains, so they must be skimmed frequently.

After a fermentation is complete and the liquid part of the mash is removed and distilled, an equal amount of new grain is added to the next batch as was skimmed from the previous batch. This way the spent grain is removed from each batch and new grain is added to replace it, which sets up a continuously sustainable sour-mash cycle that could theoretically be repeated indefinitely.

There doesn't appear to be any limit to the number of iterations that can be done using the continuous sour-mash cycle. In fact, the flavour of the whiskey seems to improve from one iteration to the next. The author experimented with twelve iterations and the only indications were improved flavour, there were no signs of degraded fermentation or loss of yeast viability.

No doubt, most of the improvement in flavour is due to the repeated recycling of the backset. Evidently, the backset becomes increasingly imbued with desirable flavour from one run to the next. This continual improvement in flavour appears to defy the principles of brewing science, but then the entire sour-mash process appears to defy brewing science. Accordingly, one would only expect a continuous sour-mash cycle to be sustainable for about eight, maybe ten, iterations. After numerous re-fermentations, yeast strains mutate and/or become contaminated, and the flavour profile deviates from that of the original yeast strain. In brewing, this would normally call for an end to the re-fermentation cycle so that a fresh culture of the specific yeast strain could be reintroduced in the next fermentation.

When a distiller wants to bring a continuous sour-mash cycle an end, the process of skimming and adding new grain can be stopped, and the cycle can be left to run out as with the intermittent sour-mash method. Of course, the backset from the last batch could be frozen and saved for the first iteration of the next sour-mash cycle.

A distiller will typically do enough sour-mash iterations to accumulate a desired amount of low wines and then perform a single spirit run on the total accumulation. This affords the economies of scale of doing larger runs, and it makes the begin- and end-cuts easier to judge.

OTHER CONSIDERATIONS

Rhizozyme (Koji)

"Rhizozyme" is a glucoamylase enzyme derived from a fungus called "rhizopus oryzae", which infects the rice plant. Rhizozyme is well known in Japan as "koji", which has been used for centuries to make sake. Sake is a form of wine made from rice. Calling sake "rice wine" is technically a misnomer because sake is actually a form of beer, not wine, since it's made from grain (ie. rice) and not fruit, but it's very commonly referred to as "rice wine", and it's always served as a wine.

Rice, like most grains, is comprised of a large proportion of starch and almost no sugar, so in order to ferment rice an enzyme must be introduced to break the rice starches down into sugars. The Japanese use koji as the enzyme to do this. Making sour mash has certain similarities to making sake in that straight unmalted grain is being fermented.

Experimentation has shown that the addition of ¾ tsp (4mL) of rhizozyme to the recipe for a 25L (6½ US gallon) batch of sour mash will significantly improve the uptake of the grain starches, which results in a step-feeding process of the yeast. A "step-feeding process" is the process whereby the grain starches are slowly broken down to glucose over the course of the fermentation, which slowly feeds sugar to the yeast throughout the fermentation.

Rhizozyme improves the overall efficiency of the sour mash process, and an intermittent sour-mash cycle may only take two iterations to completely exhaust the grain of its starches.

Unfortunately, rhizozyme is usually fairly difficult to buy in small quantities but some homebrew shops may carry it under the name "koji" for making sake. However, Beano works almost as well. Five drops of liquid Beano, or 3 crushed Beano tablets, added to a 25L (6½ US gallon) batch of sour mash will give very nearly the same results.

Bacterial Contamination

Bacterial contamination, particularly lactobacillus contamination, is one of the biggest problems commercial distilleries have to contend with. All bacteria in a mash are killed from the high temperatures during a typical cooker-mash process, and distilleries make sure the yeast they pitch is bacteria free, but still small amounts manage to contaminate the mashes anyway and measures are taken to control it.

However, with a no-cook sour-mash process the mash starts out with a very large dose of lactobacillus bacteria. All raw grain is covered with dormant lactobacillus and pediococcus bacteria. So, with no cooking to kill the indigenous bacteria on the grain, a sour mash would be teaming with these bacteria. However, it must be part of the sour-mash process, because no prevention or precaution is ever taken to control it in any of the recipes encountered by the author, and the sour-mash whiskey turns out to be good.

Perhaps the bacteria contribute to the character of the flavour of sour-mash whiskey, and the only adverse effect would be a lower yield than if the bacteria were not present, since these organisms consume some of the sugars in the mash.

Yeast Mutation

As with bacterial contamination, yeast mutation doesn't appear to affect the quality of the sour-mash whiskey. There's no doubt that yeast mutation and bacterial contamination are taking place, but they don't seem to have any deleterious effects on the flavour profile of the whiskey. Evidently, the flavour profile of sour-mash whiskey is not as dependent on the fermentation characteristics as other beverages such as beers, wines, or whiskies made by other methods are.

CHAPTER 14

MAKING YOUR OWN MALT

Barley malt is not readily available in some parts of the world. However, barley itself is available almost everywhere, and it's fairly easy to make it into barley malt if necessary. In fact, years ago making malt was an integral part of preparing the ingredients to make whiskey or beer.

All the Scottish malt whisky distilleries started out making their own malt, and even today there is the odd one that still does. However, on the whole, distilleries buy their malt from local maltsters.

Malt, by definition, is grain that has been sprouted and then dried in a kiln to kill the sprouting seeds and halt their growth. This is done to preserve the diastatic enzymes created during the sprouting process.

Any type of grain can be malted, but barley is by far the most popular. This is because there is an enormous demand worldwide for barley malt since it's the main ingredient in almost every type of beer. Combine this with the fact that there's very little demand for any other kind of malt.

Most homebrew shops that carry fresh barley malt will also carry wheat malt, which is used in wheat beers. Rye malt is also available for certain specialty beers. But, barley malt will invariably be the mainstay of their line of malts.

Grain-mash recipes require malt of one kind or another because it contains a family of enzymes called "amylase enzymes" that convert the starches in the grain to fermentable sugars. The amylase enzymes occur in two forms: alpha amylase that converts complex starches to simpler starches; and, beta amylase that converts the simpler starches to sugars. Collectively, these enzymes are known as "diastatic enzymes".

A kernel of barley is comprised of a husk, a germ, and an endosperm. The endosperm is the large bulbous starch portion that makes up the bulk of the barley kernel. When a seed sprouts to grow into a new barley plant, the germ begins creating enzymes to convert the starches in the endosperm to sugars to be consumed by the young plant in order to sustain it during its early formation stages until it is developed enough to produce its own food by photosynthesis. The principle behind making grain into malt is to initiate the sprouting process so the germ will create diastatic enzymes but then to halt the process while the enzymes are at the desired concentration and before the bulk of the starch in the endosperm is consumed. The resulting dried sprouted kernels are malt.

Commercial maltsters produce extremely high quality malts and at very affordable prices, so there's very little reason for anyone who has ready access to these malts to make their own. However, if malt is not available where you live, or if you have an abundant supply of barley, for example, if you live on a grain farm, then barley malt can be made by the process detailed below.

MAKING BARLEY MALT

The Grain

The barley must be living seed barley capable of sprouting. 2-row or 6-row are both fine, but 6-row tends to yield more diastatic enzymes per kilogram of malt. It must be whole food-grade barley that hasn't been treated in any way, either mechanically or chemically. Some barley is treated with chemicals to protect it from mildew and rot. This will NOT do.

The best barley for malting are the kernels that are of a fairly uniform size, and are plump and healthy looking. Malting barley, in general, tends to be the better barley seeds.

Freshly harvested grain does not sprout well. The barley should have been kept in a dry place for at least three months. This is not normally a problem with barley purchased from a supplier. Barley stored in a cool dry place with good ventilation will remain viable for years.

The grain must be free of unwanted debris such as chaff, dust, straw, or underdeveloped kernels. As a general rule, such unwanted debris will float, so when water is added to the grain to steep it, the unwanted debris will float and can easily be removed. The living barley kernels will sink.

If the barley you buy is food grade, it will most likely already be clean.

Steeping the Grain

The barley needs to be steeped in water until it has absorbed enough moisture to germinate. It must also be provided adequate oxygen for its metabolic processes and to eliminate any build up of carbon dioxide. To do this, completely immerse the barley in water, for example, in a pail. The water must be changed three times daily, allowing the grain to drain and sit for about an hour at each changing. The grain should be gently stirred once or twice a day as well.

Depending on the grain and the temperature of the water, the first signs of small white rootlets will appear at one end of the grains after about five to seven days. This is the time when the steeping is finished. It's quite important that the grain be taken out of the water at the first sign of these rootlets. The kernels of barley will have swelled to about 150% of their original size.

Germinating the Grain

Germination should be done in square wooden trays about 8 or 10 cm (3 or 4") deep with stainless steel screen mesh as the floor of each tray. Such trays are very easy and cheap to make, and they should be shimmed at the bottom to raise them up so they don't form an air seal on the floor.

The wet grain should be placed in the trays about 5 cm (2") deep, and they should be germinated at between 10 and 15°C (50 and 60 °F). Warmer temperatures will work but the germination will be too quick and the rate of germination will tend to be uneven from kernel to kernel.

The grain should be turned by hand about three times per day. Depending on the humidity and temperature there should be enough moisture in the grain to last until the germination is complete. However, if you feel the grain is drying out and the sprouting is slowing down, you can sprinkle the grain with water to keep it growing.

While the germination is taking place, you need to watch the development of the acrospires of the kernels. The acrospire is the early formation of the stem of the plant. At the germination stage the acrospires can be seen under the husks of the kernels as a sort of bulge developing on the side of each kernel. Until you've learned to recognize the acrospires from outside the kernels, you can break a kernel apart and see the yellowish stem developing inside. Once you've seen the kernels broken apart a few times you'll know exactly what the acrospires look like from outside the kernel.

It's important that you not mistake the acrospires from the rootlets. The rootlets, which are the early formation of the roots of the plants, develop outside the husks right from the outset, where the acrospires begin growing inside the husks.

For making whiskey, you want malt that's fully modified. Fully modified malt has more diastatic enzymes than lesser-modified malts. Fully modified malt means that the sprouts have developed to the extent that the acrospires are the full length of the barley kernels. So, as you observe the development of the acrospires each day determine when the average length of the acrospires is between ¾ and the full length of the kernels. The kernels won't all sprout at the exact same rate, so that's why you have to determine an average acrospire length. Some will be a little longer and some will be shorter. This is not a problem.

This germination process will take about a week or ten days to reach an average of full modification.

Drying the Malt

At this point you want to dry the malt out and kiln it to kill the sprouts so they stop growing. It's very important, however, to make sure you don't heat the malt too hot and destroy the diastatic enzymes.

If you have hot dry weather, you can spread the malt out on something like a plastic sheet and let the sun dry it out for a day or two. If spread out nice and thin, a good eleven hours in a hot sunny day should be enough to dry the malt out.

At this point, if you were going to use the malt right away, the dried malt could be crushed and used to make a whiskey mash with no further processing. However, if you were intending on keeping the malt for any length of time, you would have to kiln it after drying it.

If you don't have hot dry weather, you can simply move on to the kilning cycle, it'll just take longer without sun drying.

You can kiln the malt by spreading it at a depth of 2½ cm (1") or less on metal cookie sheets and placing them in an oven set at 40 or 50°C (105 or 120 °F). It's very important that the malt not be heated hotter than this. Continue to heat the malt in the oven at this temperature for about 15 hours, turning it over and mixing it up two or three times throughout the kilning cycle.

Since oven thermostats are not particularly accurate, you should use a laboratory thermometer to adjust the oven temperature before the malt is placed in it. Put a thermometer in a small jar full of water and place it in the oven, set the oven to 40 or 50°C (105 or 120°F) and check the thermometer after about ten or fifteen minutes. If the temperature is high or low, adjust the oven temperature control slightly one way or another and check the thermometer again after a few minutes. Repeat this until the oven temperature is holding steadily within the acceptable range, and then place the malt in the oven.

Depending on how much malt there is and whether it was sun dried or not, it will take from 15 to 25 hours to dry out completely.

To test the malt for dryness, bite into a kernel, the malt should be crunchy and powdery, and dry right through to the centre.

After the malt is dry it must be stripped of its culms (ie. the dried brittle rootlets) and any overgrown acrospires. This can easily be done by hand if there's only a small amount of malt, but larger quantities require a different approach.

One good way is to place the malt in a pillowcase and tie it shut in such a way that there's lots of room for the malt to rattle around inside. Then vigorously bang it against a tabletop for a few minutes.

You can also place the pillowcase, or two such pillowcases, in a clothes dryer with the air and heat turned off, and tumble them for about ten minutes. You'll want to make sure the pillowcases are securely tied if you do this because if one breaks open it will be a very long and tedious job to gather up all the malt from the inside of the dryer.

After this, return the malt to the germination boxes to screen the culms and debris from the grains.

Malt should be stored in a dry place, and cool if possible. Also, malt must be crushed before it can be used. Whole, uncrushed malt will not release its enzymes and starches to the mash water.

If the humidity is high where you live, then you will have to store the grain in airtight containers to prevent the grain from absorbing moisture from the air.

Finally, malt benefits by being matured for a couple of months after it's been kilned before using it for mashing, and if it's kept dry it'll remain viable for years. However, it can be used right away if required.

MAKING A WOODEN KILN

If it's necessary to make larger amounts of malt on an ongoing basis, a proper wooden kiln can be built by making a blower box that's exactly the same dimensions as the germination boxes, except with a solid bottom and four times as high. Lower down inside the box mount an electric blower with an air inlet cut into the side of the box.

Mount a digital probe thermometer on the outside of the box with the probe leading into the box, and mount a switch in a surface-mounted switch box on the outside to turn the blower on and off.

For heat, mount three glocones on the floor of the box and wire two of them to switches in surface-mounted switch boxes on the outside beside the blower switch. The third glocone should be wired to a dimmer switch in a surface-mounted switch box beside the other switches. Mounted on the outside of the blower box at this point you should have: a switch for the blower; two switches for two of the glocones; a dimmer switch for the third glocone; and a digital probe thermometer gauge.

On the inside of the blower box, near the wall where all the switches are mounted, a curved heat deflector fashioned from sheet metal should be mounted.

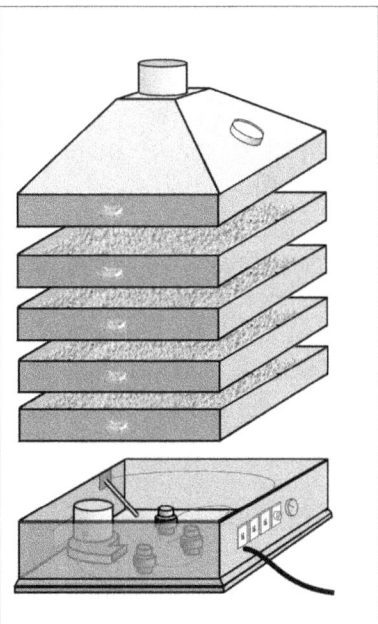

Malt Kiln

The separate switches for the glocones are so the temperature can be regulated. The dimmer switch on one of them gives a fine-tuning control.

If you can't get glocones, you can use an electric stove element or any other temperature-controllable heater. Of course, it's important that any heater used in this capacity be installed in a manner that ensures that it won't start a fire.

A strip of felt should be glued to the top edges of all the walls of the blower box and all of the screened germination boxes, to make an airtight seal.

The screened germination boxes can now be stacked on top of the blower box and serve as kiln trays.

Finally, another box must be made to serve as a lid. It should be open at the bottom but closed at the top except for a 10 to 13 cm (4 to 5 inch) vent hole, and it should be about three times the height of one of the germination boxes. It can be useful to mount a flexible clothes-dryer duct vent to the vent hole so the hot humid air can be exhausted to the outside of the building.

A digital probe thermometer must be mounted in the top box to measure the temperature of the air exiting the system.

This top box can be made in a sort of pyramid shape, thereby funneling the air to the top vent hole for added efficiency.

To operate the kiln, stack the screened germination boxes with the wet grain on the blower box and stack the top box on the top germination box. Ensuring the boxes are all making an airtight seal with each other, turn on the blower and the glocones. Let it run for a few minutes and then adjust the glocones so that the thermometer on the blower box reads 50°C (120°F).

Initially, the thermometer in the top box will read about 27 or 32°C (80 or 90°F), but as the grain dries out the temperature will rise to about 43°C (110°F). At this point the malt should be dry enough to be placed in storage. Depending on the amount of grain and whether it was sun dried or not, this will take between 15 and 25 hours.

MAKING CORN MALT

Although corn is not normally regarded as a malting grain, it makes just as good a diastatic malt as barley or wheat.

Probably the most popular reason for using corn malt is having a large supply of corn on hand the way a corn farmer would have, so making corn malt would be by far the most economical choice for obtaining malt for mashing.

Another reason for wanting to use corn malt is to produce a corn mash that's 100% corn. Some distillers prefer to avoid the addition of a different grain like barley malt. However, corn malt is often not readily available because there's very little demand for it, so making

Chapter 14 Making Your Own Malt

your own is sometimes the only way to get it. And, this can be done by the process explained below.

The Corn

As with barley, the corn must be seed corn capable of sprouting, it must not have been treated in any way, either mechanically or chemically. It's important to keep in mind that a lot of strains of corn are hybrid strains and they will not sprout or grow, so the corn must be explicitly designated as seed.

Steeping the Corn

Place the corn is a pail of water to steep. The water must be changed two or three times per day in order to provide adequate oxygen and to eliminate built-up carbon dioxide.

Small white rootlets will appear after about five days. At this point, drain the water from the corn, it's now ready for the germination step.

There's an ingenious method that can be used to accomplish the steeping if you're near a river or lake with clean potable water. Seed corn often comes in porous cloth sacks like burlap, or a plastic-weave material. Take a sharp knife and make numerous holes all over the sack so water can freely flow through to the corn. The entire unopened sack can then be placed in a river or lake for about five days. The natural movement of the water will keep the water around the corn nice and fresh, eliminating the need to change the water. After about five days when small white rootlets have sprouted, the sack can be removed from the water and the corn can be moved to the germination step.

Germinating the Corn

Germination can be done in square wooden trays as described in the section on *Making Barley Malt*. The corn should not be piled more than 5 cm (2") deep, and the temperature should be kept between 10 and 15°C (50 and 60°F). Warmer temperatures will work but the germination will be too quick and the rate of germination will tend to be uneven from kernel to kernel. The corn should be turned two or three times per day, and it will need to be kept moist. Unlike barley, the corn won't hold the moisture as well, so it will require regular watering.

As with barley, the progress of the germination is determined by observing the development of the acrospires. With corn, the acrospires (ie. the developing stems, not the rootlets) will begin inside the kernels and will require a close look to see.

The germinating corn will be at optimum enzyme levels when the sprouts are at full modification, which is when the average length of the acrospires is approximately the full length of the kernels. The kernels won't sprout at exactly the same rate so the germination should be continued until the average acrospire length is between ¾ and the full length of the kernels.

Some people don't judge the modification levels by observing the acrospire development, they just go by the length of the rootlets. They determine the end of the germination stage to be when the rootlets are an average of between 2 cm and 2½ cm (¾ inch and 1 inch) long. However, this is not likely to be as accurate a measure of the modification level as the lengths of the acrospires.

This germination process will take about a week or ten days to reach an average of full modification.

Drying the Malt

The corn malt can dried and stripped of its culms in exactly the same way as described above for barley malt. However, corn malt will take longer to dry than barley malt. Where barley malt takes from 15 to 25 hours to dry in a malt kiln or in an oven at 49°C (120°F), corn malt will take two to three days.

Sun drying does work for corn malt just as it does for barley malt, and even though it will still be moist after sun drying, its enzyme potential will be very high and it will work excellently, but its shelf life will only be a few weeks without further drying.

The shelf life of corn malt after kilning at 49°C (120°F) will not be as long as for barley malt. To achieve a longer shelf life, a second kilning at higher temperatures is necessary, but this degrades the enzyme content to a certain extent, and most distillers use up their malt early enough in its life cycle that taking measures to extend shelf life is usually not necessary.

Corn malt should be stored in its whole-kernel form, but should be crushed finely before use.

CHAPTER 15

OTHER MASHING METHODS

This chapter describes other mashing methods than the one given in *Chapter 6 Mashing*. The method described in *Chapter 6 Mashing* employs flaked maize, which is much easier to mash than undispersed forms of corn such as corn meal or corn flour. Undispersed grains require a steep at near-boiling temperatures to completely disperse their starches in the mash water, where flaked grains do not. Also discussed here, is the mashing of other cereal grains than corn.

Flaked Grains

All flaked grains can be mashed the same as flaked maize. Flaked maize was chosen as the example simply because corn is the subject matter of this text. Examples of other flaked grains that are used to make whiskey are: flaked rye; flaked wheat; flaked barley; and, flaked oats (ie. rolled oats). Flaked oats (not popular as a whiskey grain) are called "rolled oats" and are probably never referred to as "flaked oats".

Cereal Grains

To mash cereal grains that are not flaked, they need to be steeped in near-boiling water in order to disperse their starches in the mash water. There are two ways to do this: one is to bring the mash water to boil, turn off the heat, and introduce the grain to the hot mash water; and, the other is to liquefy the grain mash with some of the malt enzymes at 68°C (155°F) for a brief liquefaction rest before bringing it to near-boiling temperatures. The reason for this is to keep the mash liquid instead of a thick porridge that is very difficult to stir while chilling to mashing temperature.

Examples of widely used cereal grains for making whiskey are: corn meal; rye meal; wheat meal; and barley meal. The flour of the same grains can also be used, but requires mixing with cold water prior to adding to hot mash water to prevent clumping.

Method

Equipment

> 34-40L pot with lid
> a large plastic or wooden stirring spoon
> a floating dairy thermometer, graduated from 0°C to 110°C (32°F to 230°F)
> pH papers, range 5.0-6.5; or a pH meter
> pH papers, range 2-12; or a pH meter
> tincture of iodine
> measuring spoons
> eye dropper

Ingredients

> 23L of fairly soft municipal tap water, eg. hardness level of 4; almost no iron; 100 ppm calcium; pH 8.5.
> 10mL (2-tsp) Gypsum ($CaSO_4$)
> 95% sulphuric acid (H_2SO_4); or citric or tartaric acid; or backset
> 8L (4Kg or 8.8 lbs) cereal grain (eg. cornmeal, rye meal, wheat meal)
> 1½L (¾Kg or 1.65 lbs) crushed 2-row or 6-row pale barley malt

Prepare 23L of pH 6 to 7 mash water as described in *Chapter 6 Mashing*. Turn the stove on high, cover the pot, and let the water heat up to the conversion strike temperature, 73°C (163°F). You will have to frequently stir the water thoroughly and measure the temperature as the water heats up until the strike temperature is reached.

When the water is at the strike temperature, turn off the heat, and stir in the cereal grain. The temperature should come to rest at about 66°C (151°F) and the mash will become a thick porridge. At this point, it's only important that the mash is under 71°C (160°F). Next, stir in about 100mL of the crushed barley malt. Cover the pot and leave it for about 20 minutes. It's helpful to stir the mash every few minutes.

At this point, the mash should be liquid and easy to stir. Turn the stove back on to high and stir continually while the heat is on to avoid scorching the grain on the bottom of the pot. It may be necessary to set the stove to a lower heat to avoid scorching if the pot doesn't have a thick aluminum plate bonded to the bottom. A mechanical stirring device is very helpful for this stage.

Continue heating and stirring until the mash comes to boil. This will take about 40 minutes with the stove set on high.

When the mash is boiling, or near boiling, turn the heat off and continue to stir for five minutes. Cover the pot and let it steep for ten minutes. Next, allow the mash to cool, or force cool with an immersion chiller, to the conversion strike temperature, 66.5°C (152°F).

Stir in the remainder of the ¾Kg of crushed barley malt. The mash temperature should rest at about 65°C (149°F). Cover the mash pot and leave it for 90 minutes or longer to convert. It's helpful to stir the mash every 15 minutes or so during the 90-minute conversion rest. The mash can even be left for eight or ten hours (eg. overnight) to cool to fermentation temperature (ie. under 38°C (100°F)). An immersion chiller can be used to force cool the mash to fermentation temperature any time after the 90-minute conversion rest is complete.

After the conversion rest, the starches should be completely converted to sugars. This can be tested for by the iodine starch test described in *Chapter 6 Mashing*.

The mash is now ready for fermentation as per *Chapter 7 Fermentation*.

Millet

Millet is a cereal grain that is very commonly used in home whiskey making, and is contended by many distillers to make the best whiskey of all the grains. Millet is a very soft grain compared to the other grains discussed above, and for that reason doesn't require as high a temperature to disperse.

To mash millet, simply heat the mash water to about 88°C (190°F), turn the heat off, and add the millet meal while vigorously stirring the mash water. The temperature will rest at about 82°C (180°F), let it steep for ten minutes then chill the mash to the conversion strike temperature, 66.5°C (152°F), and add the barley malt. Continue as per the method above for other cereal grains.

*TEMPERATURE CORRECTIONS FOR HYDROMETERS

CALIBRATED AT 60°F (15.56°C)

If Temperature is:		SG:	1010-	1030-	1040-	1050-	1060-	1070-	1080-	1090-
°F	°C	Adjust Hydrometer Reading By:								
35	2		-1	-2	-2	-2	-2	-2	-2	-3
40	4		-1	-2	-2	-2	-2	-2	-2	-2
50	10		-1	-1	-1	-1	-1	-1	-1	-1
70	20		+1	+1	+1	+1	+1	+1	+1	+2
80	27		+2	+3	+3	+3	+3	+3	+3	+3
90	32		+4	+4	+4	+4	+5	+5	+5	+5
95	35		+4	+5	+5	+5	+5	+5	+6	+6
105	40		+6	+6	+6	+6	+7	+7	+7	+7
115	45		+7	+7	+8	+8	+8	+8	+9	+9
125	50		+8	+9	+9	+9	+10	+10	+10	+11

Adjust reading; for example, reading at 80°F is 1055: add 3 = 1058

---

* Table reproduced from Appendix D of *New Brewing Lager Beer*, by Gregory J Noonan, with permission from Brewers Publications, Boulder, CO

APPENDIX B

Proof-Hydrometer Temperature Correction Table

page 1 of 4 - Correction table for an alcoholometer calibrated at 20°C (under column corresponding to mixture temperature, find measured value of ethanol concentration in % abv and read the actual concentration in the left column of the same row)

Degrees Celcius

10°	11°	12°	13°	14°	15°	16°	17°	18°	19°	20°	21°	22°	23°	24°	25°	26°	27°	28°	29°	30°
8.3	8.5	8.6	8.8	8.9	9.1	9.2	9.4	9.6	9.8	10%	10.2	10.5	10.7	10.9	11.2	11.5	11.8	12.0	12.3	12.6
9.2	9.4	9.5	9.7	9.8	10.0	10.2	10.4	10.6	10.8	11%	11.2	11.5	11.7	12.0	12.2	12.5	12.8	13.1	13.4	13.7
10.1	10.3	10.5	10.6	10.8	10.9	11.1	11.3	11.6	11.8	12%	12.3	12.5	12.8	13.0	13.3	13.6	13.9	14.1	14.4	14.7
11.0	11.2	11.4	11.5	11.7	11.8	12.1	12.3	12.5	12.8	13%	13.3	13.5	13.8	14.1	14.3	14.6	14.9	15.2	15.5	15.8
11.9	12.1	12.3	12.4	12.6	12.8	13.0	13.3	13.5	13.8	14%	14.3	14.6	14.8	15.1	15.4	15.7	16.0	16.3	16.6	17.0
12.8	13.0	13.2	13.4	13.6	13.7	14.0	14.2	14.5	14.7	15%	15.3	15.6	15.9	16.2	16.5	16.8	17.1	17.4	17.8	18.1
13.7	13.9	14.1	14.3	14.5	14.7	14.9	15.2	15.5	15.7	16%	16.3	16.6	16.9	17.2	17.5	17.9	18.2	18.5	18.9	19.2
14.6	14.8	15.0	15.2	15.4	15.6	15.9	16.2	16.5	16.7	17%	17.3	17.6	18.0	18.3	18.6	18.9	19.3	19.6	20.0	20.3
15.5	15.7	15.9	16.1	16.4	16.6	16.9	17.2	17.4	17.7	18%	18.3	18.7	19.0	19.3	19.7	20.0	20.4	20.7	21.1	21.4
16.4	16.6	16.8	17.1	17.3	17.5	17.8	18.1	18.4	18.7	19%	19.3	19.7	20.0	20.4	20.7	21.1	21.4	21.8	22.2	22.5
17.3	17.5	17.7	18.0	18.2	18.5	18.8	19.1	19.4	19.7	20%	20.3	20.7	21.0	21.4	21.7	22.1	22.5	22.9	23.2	23.6
18.1	18.4	18.6	18.9	19.1	19.4	19.7	20.0	20.4	20.7	21%	21.4	21.7	22.1	22.4	22.8	23.1	23.5	23.9	24.3	24.7
19.0	19.3	19.5	19.8	20.1	20.3	20.7	21.0	21.3	21.7	22%	22.4	22.7	23.1	23.4	23.8	24.2	24.6	25.0	25.4	25.7
19.9	20.2	20.4	20.7	21.0	21.3	21.6	22.0	22.3	22.7	23%	23.4	23.7	24.1	24.5	24.8	25.2	25.6	26.0	26.4	26.8
20.8	21.1	21.4	21.6	21.9	22.2	22.6	22.9	23.3	23.6	24%	24.4	24.7	25.1	25.5	25.8	26.2	26.6	27.0	27.5	27.8
21.6	22.0	22.3	22.6	22.9	23.2	23.6	23.9	24.3	24.6	25%	25.4	25.8	26.1	26.5	26.9	27.3	27.7	28.1	28.5	28.9
22.5	22.8	23.2	23.5	23.8	24.2	24.5	24.9	25.3	25.6	26%	26.4	26.8	27.2	27.6	28.0	28.4	28.8	29.2	29.6	30.0
23.4	23.7	24.1	24.4	24.8	25.1	25.5	25.9	26.3	26.6	27%	27.4	27.8	28.2	28.6	29.1	29.5	29.9	30.3	30.7	31.1
24.3	24.7	25.0	25.4	25.8	26.1	26.5	26.9	27.3	27.6	28%	28.4	28.9	29.3	29.7	30.1	30.6	31.0	31.4	31.8	32.2
25.2	25.6	25.9	26.3	26.7	27.1	27.5	27.9	28.2	28.6	29%	29.4	29.9	30.3	30.8	31.2	31.6	32.1	32.5	32.9	33.3
26.1	26.5	26.9	27.3	27.7	28.1	28.5	28.9	29.2	29.6	30%	30.5	30.9	31.4	31.8	32.3	32.7	33.1	33.6	34.0	34.4

Proof-Hydrometer Temperature Correction Table

page 2 of 4 - Correction table for an alcoholometer calibrated at 20°C (under column corresponding to mixture temperature, find measured value of ethanol concentration in % abv and read the actual concentration in the left column of the same row)

										Degrees Celcius										
10°	11°	12°	13°	14°	15°	16°	17°	18°	19°	20°	21°	22°	23°	24°	25°	26°	27°	28°	29°	30°
27.0	27.4	27.8	28.2	28.6	29.0	29.4	29.8	30.2	30.6	31%	31.5	31.9	32.4	32.8	33.3	33.7	34.2	34.6	35.0	35.5
27.9	28.3	28.7	29.2	29.6	30.0	30.4	30.8	31.2	31.6	32%	32.5	32.9	33.4	33.8	34.3	34.7	35.2	35.6	36.0	36.5
28.8	29.2	29.7	30.1	30.5	31.0	31.4	31.8	32.2	32.6	33%	33.5	33.9	34.4	34.8	35.3	35.7	36.2	36.6	37.1	37.5
29.7	30.2	30.6	31.0	31.5	31.9	32.3	32.8	33.2	33.6	34%	34.5	34.9	35.4	35.8	36.3	36.7	37.2	37.6	38.1	38.5
30.6	31.1	31.5	32.0	32.4	32.9	33.3	33.7	34.2	34.6	35%	35.5	35.9	36.4	36.8	37.3	37.7	38.2	38.6	39.1	39.5
31.6	32.0	32.5	32.9	33.4	33.8	34.3	34.7	35.1	35.6	36%	36.5	36.9	37.4	37.8	38.3	38.7	39.2	39.6	40.1	40.5
32.6	33.0	33.5	33.9	34.4	34.8	35.3	35.7	36.1	36.6	37%	37.5	37.9	38.4	38.8	39.3	39.7	40.2	40.6	41.0	41.5
33.5	34.0	34.5	34.9	35.4	35.8	36.3	36.7	37.1	37.6	38%	38.5	38.9	39.3	39.8	40.2	40.7	41.1	41.6	42.0	42.5
34.5	35.0	35.5	35.9	36.4	36.8	37.3	37.7	38.1	38.6	39%	39.4	39.9	40.3	40.8	41.2	41.7	42.1	42.5	43.0	43.4
35.5	36.0	36.5	36.9	37.4	37.8	38.3	38.7	39.1	39.6	40%	40.4	40.9	41.3	41.7	42.2	42.6	43.1	43.5	44.0	44.4
36.6	37.0	37.5	37.9	38.4	38.8	39.3	39.7	40.1	40.6	41%	41.4	41.9	42.3	42.7	43.1	43.6	44.0	44.5	44.9	45.3
37.6	38.0	38.5	38.9	39.4	39.8	40.3	40.7	41.1	41.6	42%	42.4	42.9	43.3	43.7	44.1	44.6	45.0	45.4	45.9	46.3
38.5	39.0	39.5	39.9	40.4	40.8	41.3	41.7	42.1	42.6	43%	43.4	43.8	44.3	44.7	45.1	45.5	46.0	46.4	46.8	47.2
39.5	40.0	40.5	40.9	41.4	41.8	42.3	42.7	43.1	43.6	44%	44.4	44.8	45.2	45.7	46.1	46.5	46.9	47.3	47.8	48.2
40.5	41.0	41.5	41.9	42.4	42.8	43.3	43.7	44.1	44.6	45%	45.4	45.8	46.2	46.6	47.0	47.4	47.9	48.3	48.7	49.1
41.5	42.0	42.5	42.9	43.4	43.8	44.3	44.7	45.1	45.6	46%	46.4	46.8	47.2	47.6	48.0	48.4	48.8	49.2	49.6	50.0
42.5	43.0	43.5	43.9	44.4	44.8	45.3	45.7	46.1	46.6	47%	47.4	47.8	48.2	48.6	49.0	49.4	49.8	50.2	50.6	50.9
43.6	44.0	44.5	45.0	45.4	45.8	46.3	46.7	47.2	47.6	48%	48.4	48.8	49.2	49.6	50.0	50.4	50.7	51.1	51.5	51.9
44.7	45.1	45.6	46.0	46.5	46.9	47.3	47.7	48.2	48.6	49%	49.4	49.8	50.2	50.6	50.9	51.3	51.7	52.1	52.5	52.9
45.8	46.2	46.7	47.1	47.5	47.9	48.4	48.8	49.2	49.6	50%	50.4	50.8	51.2	51.5	51.9	52.3	52.7	53.1	53.5	53.8
46.9	47.3	47.7	48.1	48.6	49.0	49.4	49.8	50.2	50.6	51%	51.4	51.8	52.2	52.5	52.9	53.3	53.7	54.1	54.4	54.8

Appendix B Proof-Hydrometer Temperature Correction Table   177

Proof-Hydrometer Temperature Correction Table

page 3 of 4 - Correction table for an alcoholometer calibrated at 20°C (under column corresponding to mixture temperature, find measured value of ethanol concentration in % abv and read the actual concentration in the left column of the same row)

										Degrees Celsius											
10°	11°	12°	13°	14°	15°	16°	17°	18°	19°	20°	21°	22°	23°	24°	25°	26°	27°	28°	29°	30°
48.0	48.4	48.8	49.2	49.6	50.0	50.4	50.8	51.2	51.6	52%	52.4	52.8	53.1	53.5	53.9	54.3	54.7	55.0	55.4	55.8
49.0	49.4	49.9	50.3	50.7	51.1	51.5	51.9	52.2	52.6	53%	53.4	53.8	54.1	54.5	54.9	55.3	55.6	56.0	56.4	56.7
50.1	50.5	50.9	51.3	51.7	52.1	52.5	52.9	53.2	53.6	54%	54.4	54.7	55.1	55.5	55.8	56.2	56.6	57.0	57.3	57.7
51.1	51.5	51.9	52.3	52.7	53.1	53.5	53.9	54.2	54.6	55%	55.4	55.7	56.1	56.4	56.8	57.2	57.5	57.9	58.3	58.6
52.2	52.6	53.0	53.3	53.7	54.1	54.5	54.9	55.3	55.6	56%	56.4	56.7	57.1	57.4	57.8	58.1	58.5	58.9	59.2	59.6
53.2	53.6	54.0	54.4	54.7	55.1	55.5	55.9	56.3	56.6	57%	57.4	57.7	58.1	58.4	58.7	59.1	59.5	59.8	60.2	60.6
54.2	54.6	55.0	55.4	55.8	56.1	56.5	56.9	57.3	57.6	58%	58.3	58.7	59.0	59.4	59.7	60.1	60.5	60.8	61.2	61.5
55.3	55.7	56.1	56.4	56.8	57.2	57.5	57.9	58.3	58.6	59%	59.3	59.7	60.0	60.4	60.7	61.1	61.4	61.8	62.1	62.5
56.4	56.8	57.1	57.5	57.9	58.2	58.6	58.9	59.3	59.6	60%	60.3	60.7	61.0	61.4	61.7	62.1	62.4	62.8	63.1	63.4
57.4	57.8	58.2	58.5	58.9	59.3	59.6	60.0	60.3	60.7	61%	61.3	61.7	62.0	62.4	62.7	63.0	63.4	63.7	64.1	64.4
58.5	58.9	59.2	59.6	59.9	60.3	60.6	61.0	61.3	61.7	62%	62.3	62.7	63.0	63.4	63.7	64.0	64.4	64.7	65.0	65.4
59.5	59.9	60.3	60.6	61.0	61.3	61.7	62.0	62.3	62.7	63%	63.3	63.7	64.0	64.3	64.7	65.0	65.4	65.7	66.0	66.4
60.6	60.9	61.3	61.6	62.0	62.3	62.7	63.0	63.3	63.7	64%	64.3	64.7	65.0	65.3	65.7	66.0	66.4	66.7	67.0	67.4
61.6	62.0	62.3	62.7	63.0	63.3	63.7	64.0	64.3	64.7	65%	65.3	65.7	66.0	66.3	66.7	67.0	67.4	67.7	68.0	68.4
62.6	63.0	63.3	63.7	64.0	64.3	64.7	65.0	65.3	65.7	66%	66.3	66.7	67.0	67.4	67.7	68.0	68.4	68.7	69.0	69.4
63.7	64.0	64.3	64.7	65.0	65.3	65.7	66.0	66.3	66.7	67%	67.3	67.7	68.0	68.4	68.7	69.0	69.4	69.7	70.0	70.4
64.7	65.0	65.4	65.7	66.0	66.4	66.7	67.0	67.3	67.7	68%	68.3	68.7	69.0	69.4	69.7	70.0	70.4	70.7	71.1	71.4
65.7	66.0	66.4	66.7	67.0	67.4	67.7	68.0	68.3	68.7	69%	69.3	69.7	70.0	70.4	70.7	71.0	71.4	71.7	72.1	72.4
66.7	67.0	67.4	67.7	68.0	68.4	68.7	69.0	69.3	69.7	70%	70.3	70.7	71.0	71.4	71.7	72.1	72.4	72.7	73.1	73.4
67.7	68.0	68.4	68.7	69.0	69.4	69.7	70.0	70.3	70.7	71%	71.3	71.7	72.0	72.4	72.7	73.1	73.4	73.7	74.1	74.4
68.7	69.0	69.4	69.7	70.0	70.4	70.7	71.0	71.3	71.7	72%	72.3	72.7	73.0	73.4	73.7	74.1	74.4	74.7	75.1	75.4

Proof-Hydrometer Temperature Correction Table

page 4 of 4 - Correction table for an alcoholometer calibrated at 20°C (under column corresponding to mixture temperature, find measured value of ethanol concentration in % abv and read the actual concentration in the left column of the same row)

10°	11°	12°	13°	14°	15°	16°	17°	18°	19°	20°	21°	22°	23°	24°	25°	26°	27°	28°	29°	30°
69.7	70.0	70.3	70.7	71.0	71.3	71.7	72.0	72.3	72.7	73%	73.3	73.7	74.0	74.4	74.7	75.1	75.4	75.7	76.1	76.4
70.7	71.0	71.3	71.7	72.0	72.3	72.7	73.0	73.3	73.7	74%	74.4	74.7	75.0	75.4	75.7	76.1	76.4	76.7	77.1	77.4
71.7	72.0	72.3	72.7	73.0	73.3	73.7	74.0	74.3	74.7	75%	75.4	75.7	76.1	76.4	76.7	77.1	77.4	77.7	78.1	78.4
72.7	73.0	73.3	73.7	74.0	74.3	74.7	75.0	75.3	75.7	76%	76.4	76.7	77.1	77.4	77.7	78.1	78.4	78.7	79.1	79.4
73.7	74.0	74.3	74.7	75.0	75.3	75.7	76.0	76.3	76.7	77%	77.4	77.7	78.1	78.4	78.7	79.1	79.4	79.7	80.1	80.4
74.6	75.0	75.3	75.7	76.0	76.3	76.7	77.0	77.3	77.7	78%	78.3	78.7	79.0	79.4	79.7	80.1	80.4	80.7	81.0	81.4
75.6	76.0	76.3	76.7	77.0	77.3	77.7	78.0	78.3	78.7	79%	79.3	79.7	80.0	80.4	80.7	81.0	81.4	81.7	82.0	82.3
76.6	77.0	77.3	77.7	78.0	78.3	78.7	79.0	79.3	79.7	80%	80.3	80.7	81.0	81.3	81.7	82.0	82.3	82.6	83.0	83.3
77.6	78.0	78.3	78.7	79.0	79.3	79.7	80.0	80.3	80.7	81%	81.3	81.7	82.0	82.3	82.6	83.0	83.3	83.6	83.9	84.2
78.7	79.0	79.3	79.7	80.0	80.3	80.7	81.0	81.3	81.7	82%	82.3	82.7	83.0	83.3	83.6	83.9	84.2	84.5	84.8	85.1
79.7	80.0	80.4	80.7	81.0	81.4	81.7	82.0	82.4	82.7	83%	83.3	83.6	83.9	84.3	84.6	84.9	85.2	85.5	85.8	86.1
80.7	81.1	81.4	81.7	82.1	82.4	82.7	83.0	83.4	83.7	84%	84.3	84.6	84.9	85.2	85.5	85.8	86.1	86.4	86.7	87.0
81.8	82.1	82.4	82.8	83.1	83.4	83.7	84.1	84.4	84.7	85%	85.3	85.6	85.9	86.2	86.5	86.8	87.0	87.3	87.6	87.9
82.8	83.2	83.5	83.8	84.1	84.5	84.8	85.1	85.4	85.7	86%	86.3	86.6	86.9	87.1	87.4	87.7	88.0	88.3	88.5	88.8
83.9	84.3	84.6	84.9	85.2	85.5	85.8	86.1	86.4	86.7	87%	87.3	87.6	87.8	88.1	88.4	88.6	88.9	89.2	89.4	89.7
85.1	85.4	85.7	86.0	86.3	86.6	86.9	87.2	87.4	87.7	88%	88.3	88.5	88.8	89.1	89.3	89.6	89.8	90.1	90.3	90.6
86.2	86.5	86.8	87.1	87.4	87.6	87.9	88.2	88.5	88.7	89%	89.3	89.5	89.8	90.0	90.3	90.5	90.8	91.0	91.2	91.5
87.3	87.6	87.9	88.2	88.4	88.7	89.0	89.2	89.5	89.8	90%	90.2	90.5	90.7	91.0	91.2	91.4	91.7	91.9	92.1	92.4
88.4	88.7	89.0	89.3	89.5	89.8	90.0	90.3	90.5	90.8	91%	91.2	91.5	91.7	91.9	92.2	92.4	92.6	92.8	93.1	93.3
89.6	89.8	90.1	90.4	90.6	90.9	91.1	91.3	91.6	91.8	92%	92.2	92.4	92.7	92.9	93.1	93.3	93.5	93.8	94.0	94.2
90.7	91.0	91.2	91.4	91.7	91.9	92.1	92.4	92.6	92.8	93%	93.2	93.4	93.6	93.8	94.1	94.3	94.5	94.7	94.9	95.1

APPENDIX C

SPIRIT-RUN RECORD

TIME	Rate of flow (ml/min)	PHASE	Amount Collected (ml)	Amount Collected (Corrected to 100% alc)	Amount Left (ml of 100% alc/vol)	Stillhead Temp °C	% Alcohol of Emerging Distillate	% Alcohol of Aggregate

BIBLIOGRAPHY

Dabney, Joseph E. *Mountain Spirits*
Asheville, NC: Bright Mountain Books, 1974

Murtagh & Associates *The Alcohol Textbook*
Second Edition, Nottingham University Press 1999

Nixon & McCaw. *The Compleat Distiller*
The Amphora Society, 2001
www.amphora-society.com

Noonan, Gregory J. *New Brewing Lager Beer*
Boulder, CO: Brewers Publications, 1996

Stone, John. *Making Gin & Vodka*
www.gin-vodka.com, 1997

The Association of Brewers, www.beertown.org
The Journal of The American Homebrewers Association
Various issues of *Zymurgy Magazine*, Boulder, CO

Walstad, J.W. *Simple Sour Mash to Simple Alcohol Fuel*
Seattle WA: The Revenoor Stills Co. Ltd, 1979

INDEX

A

Acetone 92
Acidity 58
Acrospire 160
Acrylic 26, 49, 97
Aerating 84
Aeration stone 84
Aerobic 75
Alcohol 9, 75
Alcohol content 80
Alcohol percentage 85
Alcoholic beverages 3
Aldehydes 92
Alkalinity 58
Alpha-galactosidase 62
Amino acids 75
Amylase 70
    Alpha 67, 70
    Beta 67, 70
Amylase enzymes 157
Amylo-glucosidase 62
Anaerobic 75
Anode 35
Appalachian frontier 9
Aquarium pump 84
Aqua-vitae 10
Aqueous solution 26, 58
Azeotrope 90

B

Backset 131, 145
Backset and pH 132
Bacterial contamination 155
Baffle plates 88
Barley 56
Barley malt 56, 68, 72
Barley malt, how to make 157
Barley meal 169
Beano 63, 155
Beer 3
Beer stripper 51
Beer stripping 99
Beer-stripping 91
Bicarbonates 58
Blending 110
Boiler 34
Boiling point 4, 87
Bourbon 20
Bourbon mash recipe 140
Brandy 88
Brix Balling 78

C

Calcium carbonate 58, 65
Calcium content 58
Calcium hydroxide 59
Calcium oxide 59
Calcium sulphate 58, 64
Carbon dioxide 75
Carbonates 58
Cereal grains 169
Column still 88
Condenser coil 88
Congeners 3, 91
Continuous-run 89
Conversion 73
Cooker-mash 145
Copper scrubbers 47
Corn feints 108
Corn flour 55, 169
Corn malt, how to make 164
Corn mash 71, 82
Corn meal 169
Corn silo 142
Corn squeezins' 142
Corn whiskey 7, 107
Cornmeal 55
Crushed limestone 59
Culms 162
Cut
    Begin-cut 93, 95, 105
    End-cut 93, 107

D

Decoction 169
Deionized water 68, 110
Dextrins 63, 70, 77
Diastatic enzymes 56, 157
Diluting 110, 126

Dilution formula 110, 126
Dimmer switch 39, 113
Distillation 4, 87
   Fractional..................................5
   Simple.......................................5
Distillation Methods 101
Distilled water 59, 68
Drain-hose 28
Draining..48
Draining and flushing.................109
Dried Malt Extract......................137

E

Electrical timer 37
Electric-clothes-drier socket 52
Electric-stove socket.....................52
Endosperm............................56, 158
Enzymes 56, 62, 67
Equilibration phase 91, 121
Equilibrium....................................89
Esters 5, 77, 92
Estimated run time......................121
Ethanol..87
Ether linkage..................................67
Ethyl alcohol....................................5

F

Feints 93, 95, 97
Fermentable substrate 3
Fermentation.............................5, 75
Fermenter..82
Fermenters 24
Filler-hose......................................28
Filling 48
Finished whiskey 92
Flaked barley 169
Flaked maize................55, 72, 169
Flaked oats...................................169
Flaked rye 141, 169
Flaked wheat................................169
Flavour-positive...........................104
Flow rate 105, 109, 123
Flushing..49
Flushing-hose 28
Force cool.......................................83
Foreshots..................................5, 92
Foreshots phase 105, 122
Fractionating still..........6, 23, 32, 88
Emulating a pot sitll................112
Fractionating-still method...........104
Freezing mash..............................130
Fusel alcohols 5, 32
Fusel oils..5

G

Germ...158
Gin..23, 88
Glucoamylase 63
Glucose...67
Gooseneck......................................23
Gooseneck still..............................88
Grain pump....................................83
Grain-neutral................................111
Grist mill..20
Gypsum........................58, 64, 72

H

Hangovers..5
hard water 126
Hard water 110
Heads..5, 92
Heads phase 105, 122
Heat control 113
Heat exchanger 43
Height of the spirit still 46
History of corn whiskey.................9
Hot water heater......................34, 51
Husk..158
Hydrolysis......................................67
Hydrometer.....................25, 78, 82
Hydrometer cylinder...............26, 95

I

Immersion chiller....................28, 83
Immersion heater 37, 52
Infusion-mash................................72
Ingredients 55
Intensity of flavour 111
Iodine starch test...........................70
Iron content...................................58
Ivory Soap test............................147

K

Koji..63, 154

L

Lactobacillus 155
Lead-free plumbing solder 34
Liebig condenser 42
Liquification 67
Low wines 91, 97

M

Malt 56, 157
   Drying 161
   Fully modified 160
Malt extract 56, 136
Malt kiln 162
Malt whiskey 132, 136
Malt-extract 137
Malting barley 158
Maltsters 158
Mapping factor 104
Mash water 68, 73
Mash-extract efficiency 133
Mashing 67
Mashing back 145
Mashing methods, other 169
Mashing vessel 24
Measuring alcohol content 97
Methanol 92
Middle run 5
Middle-run 92
Middle-run phase 107, 123
Millet 172
Monongahely rye 16
Mountain Spirits 7
Municipal tap waters 59

N

Needle valve 42
Nitrogen 75
No-cook mashing 145

O

Oak barrels 6, 20, 111, 127
Old-time distillers 146
Originating Gravity (OG) 78, 82
Other whiskey recipes 129
Oxygen 76, 84

P

Packing 47
Peat 132, 138
Peat-smoked malt 138
Pediococcus 155
Percent alcohol 98
Permease 77
pH 26, 58, 68, 146
pH meter 26, 68
pH papers 27, 68
Poit du 10
Polysaccharides 63, 70, 77
Pot still 4, 23, 88
Poteen 10
Potential-alcohol scale 80
Potentiometer 38, 113
Pot-still method 112
Precipitated chalk 58, 65, 69
Primary distillation 91
Primary fermentation 76
Prohibition 7
Proof 98
Proof hydrometer 25, 97
Pure corn whiskey 111
Pure ethanol distillation 119
Purge mode 93
Purge phase 108

Q

Queen's own cask 96

R

Racking cane 25
Rack-renting 12
Recirculating Infusion Mash
   Systems (RIMS) 83
Rectifying alcohol 119
Redistill 119
Reflux 90
Reflux column 40
Reflux ratio 104
Refractometer 78, 82, 98
Residue 108
Rhizopus oryzae 154
Rhizozyme 63, 154
Rolled oats 169
Rum 88
Rye 56

Rye malt 57, 141
Rye mash recipe 140
Rye meal 169

S

Saccharification 67
Sake 63, 154
Scotch whisky 132
Scots-Irish 10
Secondary fermentation 76
Separation 87, 90
Silver-soldering 43
Siphon starter 28, 97
Siphon tube 25
Source waters 59
Sour-mash cycle
    Continuous 153
    Intermittent 149
Sour-mash whiskey 145
Sparge water 135
Sparging 58
Special Reserve 96
Specific gravity 77
Specific Gravity (SG) 78, 82
Spirit still 31, 96
Spirit-run 91
Spirits 3
Starches 67, 71
Still 4, 88
Stillhead 41
Stills
    Burner-top models 113
Storage 111, 127
Straining the mash 80, 85
Structured packing 47
Substrate 75
Sulphates 58
Sulphides 33
Sulphuric acid 64, 69, 72
Summary of procedures 115

T

Table 1 102
Table 2,3 103
Table 4 125
Tails 5, 92
Tails buffer 123
Tails phase 107, 123

Teflon tape 34
Temperature 1, 70
Terminating Gravity (TG) 79, 85
Thermistor 38
Thermometer 24, 45, 82
Thermostat 35
Thin mash 7
Thin-mash recipe 129
Transfer hoses 28
Transferring low-wines to still 97
Transferring the mash to the still .. 97
Transition points 108

U

Uisge-betha 10
Ulster Presbyterians 10
Un-malted rye 141

V

Vapours 88
Variac 39
Vodka 3, 23, 88

W

Water 58
Water jacket 88
Water solenoid 38
Wheat 56
Wheat malt 57
Wheat meal 169
Wheat-malt extract 138
Whiskey 4, 10
Whiskey distillation 91
Whiskey Rebellion 18
Whiskey still 88
Wine 3

Y & Z

Yeast 75, 82
    Bakers' 60
    Brewers' 60
    Distillers' 60
    Pure 60
    Turbo 61
    Whiskey 61
Yeast mutation 156
Zymase 75

www.ingramcontent.com/pod-product-compliance
Lightning Source LLC
Chambersburg PA
CBHW060314240426
43661CB00059B/2760